VENICE

VENICE

Jonathan Keates

Illustrated by
John Lawrence

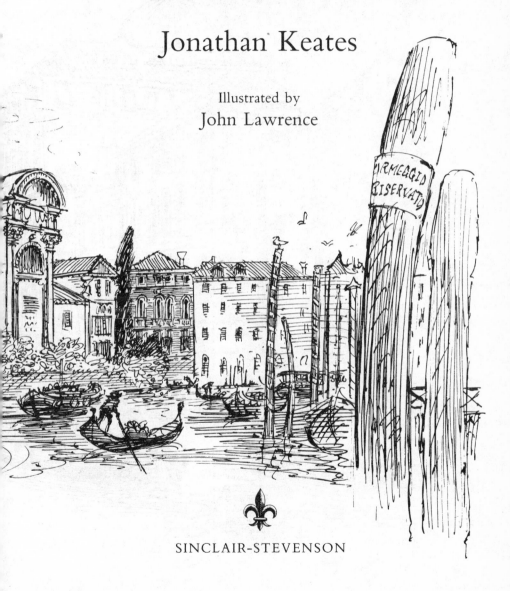

SINCLAIR-STEVENSON

To Gianni Guidetti again

The endpapers show a detail of 'View Towards Murano
from the Fondamenta Nuove' by Canaletto,
which is reproduced by gracious permission of
Her Majesty The Queen.

First published in Great Britain in 1994
by Sinclair-Stevenson
an imprint of Reed Consumer Books Ltd
Michelin House, 81 Fulham Road, London SW3 6RB
and Auckland, Melbourne, Singapore and Toronto

A CIP catalogue record for this book
is available from the British Library
ISBN 1 85619 449 3

Phototypeset by Intype, London
Printed and bound in Great Britain
by Clays Ltd, St Ives plc

Contents

1 : The Eldest Child of Liberty   1

2 : Pax Tibi Marce   19

3 : In Cannaregio   49

4 : To Byzantium and Back   77

5 : Painters' Venice   107

6 : The Surprise of the Salute   138

7 : To the Islands   167

Index   191

AUTHOR'S NOTE

I did not intend to write this book as an independent
text. It was initially designed to accompany a set of
photographs of Venice in a series that the original
publishers cut short while I was finishing the last
chapter. The proposed arrangement was as a sequence
of Venetian walks, and I have chosen to preserve
this without significant changes. In the apparently
deathless tradition of English know-it-alls sounding
off on Venice, which stretches back via Horatio
Brown and Augustus Hare to Evelyn and Coryate,
mine is an entirely personal view of the city, and I
offer no apology for the indulgence of my
enthusiasms and prejudices.

1 : The Eldest Child of Liberty

'Everything about Venice', wrote Lord Byron, 'is like a dream.' His words reflect an essential truth, that the city is, and has always been, as strong in the imagination as in reality. Optimism as much as practical need originally established a settlement on the mudbanks of a lagoon, in the Adriatic waters of northern Italy. In its great days as the capital of an independent republic, it was the abstract concept of Venice as 'the eldest child of Liberty', inviolate, perfect, 'La Serenissima', the Most Serene, to which Venetians and their colonial subjects throughout the eastern Mediterranean were expected to stay loyal. When in 1848 the citizens rose in heroic revolt against the Austrians, to whom their territory had been cynically assigned after the Napoleonic War, they suffered and died for the image of their city as a freeborn commonwealth, great once again in its defiance of tyrants and invaders.

Venice belongs to everybody who has ever built on the designs shaped by their fantasy, but the kind of visions it encourages are not those of puritans, ascetics or would-be saints. As the worldliest spot on earth it offers infinite comfort to those in search of a moment's meditation which will not involve shutting out the pleasures of the senses. Henry James understood its subtle ministrations perfectly when he wrote 'The deposed, the defeated, the disenchanted, the wounded or even only the bored have seemed to find there something that no other place could give'.

Besides nurturing its own painters, musicians, dramatists and poets, the city has offered a perpetual inspiration to artists from elsewhere, summoned initially by the legendary allure created by the very name of Venice, and, once arrived, lingering in fascination at the unique idiom of Venetian life, at the singular effects of light upon the surfaces of green water and white marble, and at the intimate sense of possession and familiarity which its streets, bridges and canals so swiftly engender.

Everybody feels they own Venice, yet, since the close of the eighteenth century at least, there has always been a certain idea that in the blink of an eye La Serenissima, in all the raddled opulence of her churches and palaces, will finally slither out of sight into the engulfing waters of the lagoon. Part of the city's fascination is created by this sense of elusiveness, by the idea that since it may not be here for very much longer the place must be seized, possessed and enjoyed to the last mouthful.

The air of splendour in decay has also contributed not a little to Venice's hold on the civilized imagination. At the zenith of its political and mercantile power, visitors were suitably dazzled. 'By the name of its beauty and the merit of its elegance it could be set between the star Arcturus and the shining Pleiades,' wrote a mediaeval Irish friar, pausing here on his way to Jerusalem, while John Evelyn in 1646, looking down on it from the top of the Campanile of Saint Mark's, enthused over 'the surprising sight of this miraculous Citty, which lies in the bosome of the sea, in the shape of a lute, the numberless Islands tacked together by no fewer than 450 bridges'.

The genuinely crucial impact occurred only after all vestiges of power had been stripped from the Republic, first by Napoleon Bonaparte in 1797 and then by the Austrians, whose annexation of Venice and its territories to the Hapsburg Empire was confirmed in 1815. There is something infinitely romantic, of course, in the notion of a once-great metropolis, 'she who did hold the gorgeous East in fee', brought low and abandoned to dreams and memories. Ever since the fall of the Venetian state, this image of decadence and former glory has been shamelessly exploited, often with an almost monotonous insistence, as though there were nothing left in Venice to admire save a heap of noble ruins enmeshed in malodorous canals.

Alas, the city's modern evolution, if it can be called that, has not helped. Austrian attempts to drag Venice into the mainstream of nineteenth-century progress, with a railway link to *terra firma* and a sometimes drastic urban development programme, may have been well-meant, but alongside this went a deliberate policy, on the part of the Hapsburg government, to promote Trieste as a seaport at Venice's expense. Nor has united Italy, which she joined in 1866, been much kinder to her. Serious and continuing pollution from mainland industry has plagued the lagoon and kept up an insidious assault on the city. Depopulation remains a problem. However attractive at first the silence of Venetian streets may be, it is worth contrasting the inexorable emptiness of their shuttered windows and firmly bolted doors with the frantic, teeming intensity of life along these alleys during the eighteenth century, when the dramatist Carlo Goldoni brought such wonderfully rich slices of it onto the Italian stage. Nowadays many Venetians have fled to a less cramped existence in the utterly uninteresting mainland town of Mestre, whence they commute daily to their bars and shops in Venice itself. Some of them may actually own property in the city, but as a friend once explained to me, the complexity of Italian law means that it is actually more advantageous to leave the houses empty or rent them out at exorbitant rates to crazy foreigners than to live there yourself.

Venice needs people: not more tourists, but people who work and sleep and put down roots here, children who play in the squares, neighbours who chat across the street and keep the shops busy. At our most blasé and sophisticated, those of us who love the place can cynically declare that it would probably be a good thing if it was simply allowed to collapse altogether. Yet what a dismal betrayal of the men and women whose vision and energy shaped this amazing creation on nothing much more than a pile of mud and a handful of sticks some sixteen hundred years ago!

The foundation of Venice was the fortunate outcome of an entirely natural geographical process involving the collection of heavy deposits of silt in the waters of the northern Adriatic around the estuaries of the rivers Brenta, Piave, Tagliamento and Livenza. The resulting mudbanks soon became small islands where, during the fifth and sixth centuries, the farmers and fishermen of the Italian mainland could easily find refuge from successive waves of barbarian invaders, Goths, Vandals, Huns and Lombards, pouring down the mountain passes into the fertile plains below and laying waste the towns and cities once protected by the power of imperial Rome.

The notion of a direct link with the old Roman empire of consuls, senators and procurators was of course crucial to the subsequent myth-history and propaganda evolved by the Venetian state in its golden years during the late Middle Ages. It became *de rigueur* for the great aristocratic families, Mocenigo, Morosini, Giustiniani and others, to devise for themselves an authentic pedigree among the patrician clans of ancient Rome itself. A traditional year of foundation was established – 421 – and the founders themselves were identified as refugees from the mainland cities of Aquileia, Altinum and Concordia, utterly laid waste by the Huns.

Even if things were not quite as simple as this, by the end of the sixth century the communities which had settled around the lagoon at such places as Malamocco, Torcello and Grado were numerous enough to constitute a province of the Byzantine Empire, first under maritime tribunes and then under a single magistrate known as a *duca*, or in the more familiar Venetian

form, *doge*, the first of these, Paoluccio Anafesto, being appointed in the year 697.

Close though the links between Venice and Byzantium rapidly became, there was never any question of the island settlements truckling under in absolute subservience to an imperial power. In 809 King Pepin of the Franks, son of the great Emperor Charlemagne, brought an army into the lagoon with the aim of curbing the independence of the fledgling republic. The seat of government at Malamocco, on the long, narrow island of the Lido, suddenly seemed all too easily exposed to attack by the Frankish fleet, and the Venetians hurriedly retreated to the much safer haven of Rivus Altus, Rialto, where they successfully saw off Pepin's menaces and were never seriously threatened again by a foreign invader for another nine hundred years.

This was the first manifestation of that capacity for single-minded loyalty and courageous defiance which was to unite the citizens of Venice at the crisis points of an amazing history which now began to unfold, one of the most romantic, in its sequence of triumphs and disasters, ever to be experienced by any independent state in the annals of the inhabited world. For on that island of Rialto and its immediate neighbours there arose, in defiance of all probability, a stupendous array of marble-fronted palaces and churches, testimony to resources of wealth and power which could hardly have been envisaged by those first migrants from the crumbling mainland towns of late antiquity.

To freshen the water of the canals and carry away the refuse and sewage thrown into them from the houses along their banks, the Venetians diverted the various rivers so that, unlike other mediaeval towns perpetually plagued by noisome stenches and the perils of contagious disease, Venice remained one of the healthiest cities in Europe. Slowly the streets and open spaces were paved, bridges of wood and stone were raised across the canals, and the original settlement spread out to embrace no less than a hundred little islands, divided into six districts known as Sestieri: San Marco at the centre, Castello to the east, Cannaregio to the north, and Dorsoduro, San Polo and Santa Croce on the southern side of the main thoroughfare of Canal Grande, the Grand Canal.

Both the money which raised the early mediaeval city and the taste which decorated it derived from Venetian merchants' increasingly successful ventures into the Byzantine world of the eastern Mediterranean. An alliance against the Norman invaders of Epirus in northern Greece at the end of the eleventh century secured Venice 'most favoured nation' status at Constantinople, making her submission to imperial control merely a formality. Only when the victorious Crusaders began to establish themselves as monarchs and princes throughout the Levant did the Venetians, keen to cut out competition from their rivals in Genoa, Pisa and Lucca, start seriously pushing home their commercial advantages.

The climax of this eastward thrust was reached in 1204, when the Doge Enrico Dandolo, ostensibly in revenge for a massacre of Venetians by the Greek Emperor Manuel Comnenus some thirty years previously, diverted the latest wave of crusading forces to Constantinople and sacked the whole glorious metropolis, the wonder of Christendom, the envy of the world. Dandolo was blind and over eighty, but he was also wily and tough, a true *figlio di San Marco* (son of Saint Mark). Into Venetian hands fell not merely the stupendous treasures heaped up by a civilization which, despite the knocks it received from encroaching Arabs and Turks, was still the most sophisticated in the Mediterranean, but also the territorial spoils of empire, a scatter of Greek islands, the peninsula of Euboea (the Venetians always called it Negroponte), the coastal strip of the Peloponnese and the rich prize of Crete. The republic's badge of the winged lion holding an open book between his paws inscribed with the words *Pax Tibi Marce Evangelista* – 'Peace to thee, Mark the Evangelist' – was set in stone above castle gateways in the Mani, on windy hilltops in the Cyclades and over the portals of palaces and churches in the towns of the Dalmatian coast, and the triumph of Venice's imperial dream was matched by hard economic reality as her trading rivals, most notably the Genoese, were swept from the eastern seas.

The success of the Venetians in stamping their supremacy on the Greek world would never be total, and the native inhabitants of the Aegean archipelago scarcely learned to love their colonial masters, yet after the Turkish presence it is the imprint of the Serene Republic which bites deeper on coastal and island Greece than any other. Certain of the great patrician family names – Contarini, Foscari, Cornaro – are still to be found in the Cyclades, and this reminds us that much of the smooth running of the empire was due to the creation of a hyper-efficient bureaucracy staffed by a rigorously restricted oligarchy made up of noble clans like these.

Their names were inscribed in the Golden Book of the Republic and they spread their roots and branches throughout the Venetian domains. From among them were chosen the five hundred members of the Maggior Consiglio, the state's supreme assembly, the magistrates of the Council of Ten, the three hundred senators, the so-called colleges of the Savi, specialists in various administrative departments such as finance and the armed forces, the procurators, generals, admirals and ambassadors, all of them distinguished by their crimson robes of office, suggested partly by the Roman toga and partly by the Byzantine court uniform which had in its turn been modelled on the ceremonial mandarin costumes of imperial China.

Out of this aristocracy the Doge himself was chosen as the ultimate embodiment of subservience to the abstract ideal of the state. The purpose of the wildly complex system leading to his election, involving a whole series of committees and ballots (our English word derives directly from the little balls, *ballotti*, used by the patrician electors), was to create a depersonalized figurehead, the forerunner of a modern constitutional monarch, the symbol of ordered, stable government, with power vested in a limited electorate rather than wielded by a capricious tyrant. Once elected (and the office was seldom if ever refused) the Doge had to give up all trading activity, to renounce every form of gift and undertake not to lobby for political appointments on behalf of his own family. His presidency of the various councils was honorific and he had no voting rights. His wife the Dogaressa was likewise turned into a 'non-person', denied the gaily extravagant social round of most Venetian noblewomen and given, like her husband, the humblest of funerals.

Yet such was the political consciousness of the Venetian aristocracy that the notion of service to the republic, culminating in the paradoxical impotence of the highest position in the pyramid of government, was instinctive among patrician families, whose members went out to govern an empire which at its widest stretched from the island of Castellorizzo off the Turkish coast, as far west as the cities of Crema and Brescia lying almost at the very gates of Milan.

For one by one, throughout the fourteenth and fifteenth centuries, the towns of northeastern Italy – Padua, Verona, Vicenza, Bergamo, Treviso, Udine and others – yielded their freedom to Venice, and the seaborne city made sure of its landward approaches as well as providing its people with sufficient food from the rich farmlands of the Veneto and Lombardy. Loathed and envied by the rest of Italy (partly, one assumes, because its sophisticated internal management was so notably different from the kind of rule by dynastic tyranny operating everywhere else), Venice was continually challenged by war or conspiracy, though the lagoon itself remained inviolate and the inhabitants of the *terraferma*, the Republic's Italian domain, stayed loyal, however grudgingly, to Saint Mark's winged lion, guarding his opened book on the tops of marble columns in a score of handsome town squares.

By 1500 Venice had become the most prosperous and densely populated city in Europe. Artists from Germany and Flanders, let alone Italy itself, found generous patrons here, and the sixteenth century witnessed the flowering of pictorial, sculptural and architectural styles which mirrored the alliance between the Venetians' wealth and love of display on the one hand and a sober purity of line and form on the other. The world of traders and markets, of Shakespeare's *Merchant of Venice*, with its talk of bargains, bonds and ventures, was also that realized for us by the opulent imagination of masters such as Bellini, Giorgione, Titian, Tintoretto and Veronese.

In churches and palaces of white marble from the quarries of Istria (the coastal region of modern Slovenia) built to designs by Scamozzi or Longhena, or in country villas created by Andrea Palladio from his study of Roman architecture, the Venetians could listen to the music of the Gabrieli, of Monteverdi and Cavalli, much of it published in their city, which had become the first great capital of European printing. Passionate for novelty and spectacle, they flocked to watch players of the *commedia dell'arte*, the traditional popular theatre of masks, to enjoy puppet shows, conjurors, fortune-tellers and street musicians, to firework displays and lavish processional regattas on religious feast days, to the Republic's great state ceremonials, and to the most exotic new diversion of all, combining song, dance and spectacle, the opera, devised in Florence but perfected and given its earliest standard form by composers and poets working here in Venice.

Ironically this last great burst of artistic energy at the close of the Italian Renaissance also saw the beginning of Venice's slow decline as a European commercial power. The success of the Turks, following the fall of Constantinople in 1453, clawing away morsel after morsel of the Republic's Greek empire, was completed with the Ottoman conquest of Cyprus in 1571 and the surrender of Crete in 1669. Long before this, the Portuguese discovery of sea routes to the East had undermined the city's primacy as an *entrepôt* for Oriental trade goods, especially spices, and other nations were able to undercut its all-important lace-making and glass industries through industrial espionage.

The immense wealth accumulated and husbanded by Venice over successive centuries meant that her fall to second-, then to third-class status was exceedingly protracted and barely acknowledged by visitors to the city until the eighteenth century, when an English poet could write, half mocking, half regretful:

There Cupids ride the lion of the deeps,
Where, reft of fleets, the Adriatic main
Wafts the smooth eunuch and th'enamour'd swain.

Even if it became, as one of its patricians noted, 'just a marionette theatre', where the notorious carnival season seemed to last
a year and where a tribe of impoverished nobility ran gaming
houses to maintain their customary lifestyle, Venice was still one
of the music capitals of Europe and seemed as much in love as
ever with the beauty of a newly-frescoed ballroom, a painted
ceiling or a marble façade. Nothing, it appeared, could kill that
vitality and brio inspiring Goldoni's comedies, Tiepolo's magical
brush or Vivaldi's endlessly inventive concertos.

When the end came, on 12th May, 1797, it was as a direct
result of Venice's desperate attempts at political self-preservation
through hedging her bets in the war between Austria and revolutionary France. Through a characteristic mixture of bullying
and chicanery on the part of Napoleon, who wanted to throw
the city and its domains as a sop to the Hapsburg Emperor
Francis II, the Maggior Consiglio contrived to vote itself out of
office, a process accelerated by the false alarm occasioned by a
salute from the guns of a loyal Croat regiment drilling outside
the Doge's Palace. The fainéant nobles hurriedly doffed their
robes of state, keen to figure as egalitarian, liberty-loving 'citizens' in the approved revolutionary mode. The Republic of
Venice, in being for almost a thousand years, the longest-lasting
political entity in the history of the modern world, had been
extinguished in the space of a few minutes.

Well, perhaps not altogether. The cynical handover of Venetian
territory to the Austrians by the Treaty of Campoformio (1798),
confirmed at the Congress of Vienna in 1815, made Venice in
theory at least a sharer in the benefit of the Austro-Hungarian
empire. Whatever the repressive, anti-democratic nature of
imperial government in what was now the province of Venetia-
Lombardy, the administration seemed a good deal more just,
efficient and impartial than many others in contemporary Europe,

and sincere attempts were made by the Austrian authorities to improve the infrastructure of the city itself. Several essential features the modern resident or tourist takes for granted – a swift, convenient public transport service on the Grand Canal, a railway link with the mainland, adequate street lighting, and the host of elegant little wrought-iron bridges spanning the smaller waterways – are reminders of the happier side of *Venezia Austriaca*.

What the Hapsburgs deliberately chose to ignore was Venice's commercial role as a seaport. While their favoured Trieste flourished as a centre for Adriatic steamshipping, the erstwhile Bride of the Sea was allowed to become the ghost-town for moralizing and impression-gathering tourists which it has remained until the present day. The Austrians, by such humiliating neglect, helped to create the fantasy of vanished splendour and irredeemable decadence, the notion of Venice as a historic theme-park off which, for better or worse, the city now survives.

The lion, however, had one more roar in reserve. As the various Italian states struck out towards unification, the Venetians too rose against their imperial overlords and, in the most heroic chapter in Venice's history, threw out the Austrians and kept them at bay under harrowing siege conditions for over a year. The events and personalities of that whole splendid and terrible episode of 1848–9 are seldom dealt with by most writers on the city, but in this book at least you will find some of them mentioned at various points during your Venetian walks.

Walking, it had better be said at once, is the only practical modern way of experiencing Venice. Even before the Austrians handed it over to the kingdom of Italy in 1866, many of its canals had been filled in and paved over. The tourist city which it then definitively became was still thronged with gondolas, but since World War Two and the increase in what the Italians, with dire ambiguity, refer to as 'tourist appurtenances', in the form of myriad cheap hotels and restaurants, private boats are either small launches and motorized barges used for transporting heavy goods or else the pleasure craft and water taxis of the rich, joyriding on the lagoon or carrying some chic coterie across from the Giudecca to the delights of Harry's Bar. The number of those with private gondolas and household gondoliers can surely be counted on the fingers of one hand.

The Venetian omnibus is the *vaporetto*, no longer the steamboat implied by its name, but a motor vessel which nowadays arrives in various forms, depending on which of the different routes you happen to be following. The swiftest tend to be numbers 2 and 5, which coop up their passengers in two compartments with small windows, so those wanting to see the city and with plenty of time to spare will prefer the Accelerato, number I, which sustains its leisurely pace all the way down the Grand Canal and over to the Lido. This boat has the advantage of open decks fore and aft, and the experience of sitting out on either of these and watching the passing show of the canal or the play of light on the surface of the water between a succession of handsome palace facades is, for many, their first exhilarating encounter with the Venetian visual impact.

Private gondolas may ply no more, but there are plenty for public hire and, judging by the youth and agility of many of today's gondoliers, the business is a lucrative one, since the chink of coins and the rustle of notes have always been attractive sounds to a Venetian. If you are the kind of traveller whose soul revolts at doing what a thousand others are doing at the same time, you can always pick up the sensation of riding in a gondola by taking one of the ferries – *traghetti* – scattered along the canal and manned by two boatmen, Charons to whom a small coin is tossed and who keep up a stentorian dialogue in their gravel-voiced yet always bizarrely musical Venetian accents, as you lurch and sidle out across the water in the wash of passing motor traffic.

Once upon a time the vocal music of the gondoliers was a little more obviously melodious. Eighteenth-century travellers marvelled at their singing of whole stanzas of Tasso's great epic poem *Gerusalemme Liberata*, and Goethe, who devotes a vibrantly detailed chapter to Venice in his *Italienische Reise*, arranged for two boatmen to give him a sample performance, aware that the tradition was already falling into disuse. The custom, apparently, was for one singer to chant his verse as loudly as possible so that another, on a distant canal, would pick up the echo and throw back the next strophe. Reclining in his gondola under the full moon of a mild early autumn night, the German poet was entranced by the effect. 'The sound of their far-off voices was extraordinary, a lament without melancholy, and I was moved to tears,' he wrote, 'it is the cry of some solitary human being sent forth into the wide world till it touches the ears of another like him who is moved to answer it.'

Like everything else in Venice, the gondola has its own traditions and vocabulary, though nobody seems quite sure how its present shape evolved. Strict sumptuary laws decreed that the boats must be painted black, without any ornamentation save for a pair of seahorses in brass and the curious silver-painted prow, whose six serrations are said to represent the various quarters (*sestieri*) of the city. Formerly each gondola carried a *felze* or canopy with curtains, which made it understandably popular with lovers and conspirators. The unwritten 'do not intrude' could be aggressively reinforced, as John Evelyn once discovered. 'Conveying a gentlewoman who had supped with us to her gondola at the usual place of landing, we were shot at by two carbines from another gondola, in which were a noble Venetian and his courtezan, unwilling to be disturbed.'

Your progress down the Grand Canal is not likely nowadays to be interrupted with gunfire, and the journey offers an ideal introduction to the city's unique synthesis of the manmade and the natural, to the flesh and blood of its singular body, made of marble, brick and water. Your eye will soon grow accustomed to picking out the telling detail, a mediaeval doorway, a Renaissance balcony, carved panels of Byzantine stonework, or a pair of muscular Baroque atlanti on either side of a porch. Your memory will start to catch hold of certain familiar Venetian colours, the green of the seaweed bearding the marble foundations of the palaces, the pale salmon pink of patches of old brick, the blue and white of the mooring poles and the infinite variations in the mottling and weathering of stonework.

Assuming that, like most people, you start your journey from the vaporetto station by the Ponte degli Scalzi, on the left bank of the canal, you will find that the genuine visual peculiarity of Venice begins to emerge once you have passed the church of San Geremia a little further down on the same side. One by one the sequence of splendid patrician palaces crowds into view, and their names, Loredan, Vendramin, Foscari, Cornaro and the rest, are those you will find repeated again and again throughout Venice, along with a handful of others from that carefully limited peerage whose names were inscribed in the Republic's Golden Book, a register which Napoleon took care to burn symbolically when he conquered the city in 1797.

None of these families had titles (though many later consented to ennoblement when the Austrian Emperor offered them the chance) and all were inordinately proud. Yet their fortunes were built on commerce and the design of their palaces, however grand, always reminds you of this fact. Notice the great watergate entrance to each building, not just a spacious atrium for the reception of important guests, but a place where originally merchandise could be unloaded and stacked. Above you will catch a glimpse of pompous saloons, hung with patterned brocade, gilt-framed sconces and chandeliers fashioned in delicate fronds of coloured glass. On the rooftops stand little wooden platforms known as *altane*, where, on festive occasions such as the summer firework night of the Redentore, the Venetians sit out in the cool of the evening eating and drinking. Several of the palaces carry cone-shaped finials on their topmost parapets: these were not merely decorative, but indicated that a member of the family had been an admiral in the fleets of the Republic.

By the time you come in sight of the Rialto Bridge, the full range and diversity of Venetian architecture will have made itself felt. Much has survived from the city's earliest age of real prosperity during the twelfth and thirteenth centuries, in the form of squat Romanesque columns, rounded arches which subsequently develop a Moorish bulge, and the circular stone discs carved with peacocks, doves, lions and other symbolic forms, set here and there into the masonry. Many of the later Mediaeval palaces feature the line of tall central windows under ogival arches which, in modified forms, were to dominate the façades of houses large and small throughout Venice over successive centuries.

Just as idiosyncratic as the Venetian Gothic style was the Renaissance idiom of local architects in the age of Bellini and Giorgione at the beginning of the sixteenth century. Among this period's significant achievements is one of the most famous of all Venice's principal landmarks, spanning the Grand Canal at the first of its two main bends. Plans for a bridge to link the central islands had been devised as early as 1181, when a primitive pontoon structure was paid for with a toll on those crossing it, but a second wooden bridge collapsed in 1444 under the weight of an immense crowd gathered to watch the entrance into the city of Leonello d'Este, Marquis of Ferrara. Its replacement, which you can see in Carpaccio's painting *The Miracle of the Relic of the Cross*, was finally pulled down in 1554, and the government resolved that at last a stone bridge should provide a suitably elegant and substantial halfway mark in the course of the canal.

The Ponte del Rialto was completed in 1591 to designs by Antonio da Ponte (1512–1597), a not especially distinguished military architect, whose plan was preferred to those by more notable figures such as Vignola, Scamozzi and Palladio. The tall arcades (too tall, say some, to harmonize with the gentle arch of the bridge itself) contain shops, and the central porticoes open out onto balustrades from which you gain splendid views up and down the canal. Notice, as you approach, the cleverly conceived reliefs of the Archangel Gabriel and the Virgin Mary, forming an Annunciation group, the work of Agostino Rubini (fl. 1580–90) and the inscription assigning the bridge to the reign of Doge Pasquale Cicogna, whose surname, meaning 'stork', is figured in the canting coat of arms.

Beyond the Rialto the Grand Canal appears increasingly wider and the dimensions of its palaces become more opulent. The Palazzo Grimani, for example, a little way along the left bank from the busy *vaporetto* station near the bridge, seems just a shade too overbearing: the architect Michele Sanmicheli (1484–1559) left it incomplete at his death, and though a second floor was added, it still looks faintly as if its former owners were thinking of something more along the lines of the Tower of Babel. The designer of the topmost storey, Gian Giacomo de'Grigi (d. 1572), came from Bergamo, and created the much lovelier Palazzo Coccina Tiepolo on the opposite bank.

As you near the last bend in the canal, you pass the small Palazzo Benzon. This was once the home of Countess Marina Querini Benzon, one of the most popular Venetian hostesses of the early nineteenth century, and famous for what used politely to be known as 'the ripeness of her charms'. Between a pair of voluminous breasts she used to tuck a slice of hot *polenta*, the maize meal which replaces pasta as the farinaceous staple of Veneto peasant diet. Venetians, watching the little cloud of steam rising from her bosom, used to call out *'Ghe xe el fumeto!'* – 'There goes the little smoke!' She is said to have been beautiful at sixty, to have had an affair with Byron, who lived further down the canal in the vast Palazzo Mocenigo, and to have inspired the best-loved of all the gondoliers' songs, *La Biondina in Gondoleta*, which any self-respecting Venetian should at least know how to whistle.

With the canal curving into its final stretch, you should now be touched with something of the infection of Venice's peculiar enchantment, created, as much as anything else, by the swirl and slap of the water against the weed-grown sides of the tall palaces, by the staring whiteness of their Istrian marble walls, by the spray and curl of rippling waves around your boat and by the capricious dance of that elusive, ever-changing Venetian light. Here, all of a sudden, is the Accademia Gallery, with Her Britannic Majesty's Consulate close beside it, and the curious little cottage-like building on the other side, with its delightfully green garden stretching out to touch the stream.

Linking them is the incongruously plain wooden Ponte dell' Accademia, built in the present century as a replacement for an earlier iron structure. Standing at the top of this bridge you can look along the last glorious 'home straight' of the Canal as it debouches into the open basin in front of Saint Mark's. On your left are the restored mediaeval Palazzo Cavalli, and next to it the Palazzo Barbaro, where Henry James, as a guest of the Curtis family, worked on novels such as *The Portrait of a Lady* and *The Wings of the Dove*. On your right are the one-storey palazzo housing the Guggenheim twentieth-century art collection and the Ca'Dario, one of Venice's haunted palaces. Beyond, marking an eye-catching finish to the prospect, is the ballooning marble bulk of Santa Maria della Salute, with the island of San Giorgio hazy in the distance. You can savour this tremendous vista among the daytime crowds up and down the bridge, but I recommend you instead to come up here at midnight and see it under a full moon as the great bell of Saint Mark's begins tolling and the lights of a lonely barge cut across the blackness of the water.

2 : Pax Tibi Marce

All Italian cities begin and end in the piazza, the central square adorned with a church, a palace and a statue or two, which provides the backdrop for every kind of human activity from a romantic assignation to a bloody revolution, and Venice is no exception. Its Alpha and Omega is the most famous square in Italy and the inspiration, in layout and atmosphere, for countless others throughout the world, the Piazza San Marco, Saint Mark's Square.

This is the only piazza in the city, because every other open space in Venice is traditionally called a *campo* or field, and though Saint Mark's Square began life as a large grassy orchard on the shore of the lagoon, it has since become far too sophisticated to smack of anything specifically agricultural. Most visitors to Venice have tended to look upon it indeed as something not unlike an immense saloon with the ceiling taken off, a place devoted exclusively to the gregarious delights of watching others and being watched by them. John Ruskin's wife Effie, whose youthfully spontaneous responses to Venetian life provide an enthralling counterpart to her husband's lapidary essays on art and architecture, describes it as like 'a vast drawing room lighted enough by the gas from the arcades all round the square, under which sit all the Ladies & gentlemen at their coffee, iced water and cigars, with a dense crowd in the centre of men, women, children, soldiers, Turks, magnificent Greek costumes and sky above studded with innumerable twinkling stars'.

Nowadays the quality of the crowd is a good deal less arresting than it was in 1849 when Effie first arrived. Tourists with very low expectations of what Venice can actually offer them, an almost total ignorance of what makes the city unique and a singular lack of curiosity as to its history and culture, throng the square, scattering their refuse across its marble steps and using its pavements as a football ground and a campsite. Anyone wanting to take the measure of Venice's principal modern headache, that of its own insensate greed encouraging the wrong sort of tourism and then making angry, helpless bleatings when required to cope with the problem, need do no more than wander into Piazza San Marco on a July or August afternoon.

If, on the other hand, you want to see the square as it deserves, then I suggest – and this applies to Venice generally – that you contrive to be here at some time between late September and early April, when the trippers have fled, the noisy Italian school parties are not yet let loose, and there is still space to breathe and look without interruption. Or, if this is impossible, come into the Piazza late at night when the place is quite empty. Venice goes to bed surprisingly early, and a nocturnal stroll across the silent city, with its dramatic street lighting, is one of the minor pleasures of existence.

As you cross beneath the portico of the so-called Bocca della Piazza, 'the mouth of the square', at the eastern end, you can scarcely fail to share the sensation recalled by an Elizabethan

20

traveller Thomas Coryate, who wrote that 'at my first entrance it did even amaze or rather ravish my senses. For heere is the greatest magnificence of architecture to be seene, that any place under the sunne doth yeelde.' Looking towards Saint Mark's basilica, you find yourself shadowed by the colonnade of the square's newest section, built in 1810 by the Modenese architect Giuseppe Soli (1745–1823) under orders from Bonaparte and thus known as the Ala Napoleonica, the Napoleonic wing. This replaced one of the twenty or so Venetian churches pulled down during the nineteenth century, San Geminiano, whose original foundation plan can be seen in the pavement immediately in front of you.

The church's façade had been added in the sixteenth century by the illustrious Jacopo Tatti, the Tuscan sculptor and architect better known as Sansovino (1486–1570) from his birthplace at Monte San Savino south of Arezzo. Fleeing from the sack of Rome by the imperial troops in 1527, he settled in Venice, where the Republic, only too pleased to have acquired the services of one of the most distinguished artificers of the age, awarded him a series of exciting commissions. After a long life, apparently sustained by a vegetarian diet consisting mainly of lemons and cucumbers, he was buried in San Geminiano.

Guidebook writers have been unduly severe on the Ala Napoleonica, which, when all is said and done, imposes its own rather frigid logic on the other two wings of the square, themselves colonnaded loggias each with two floors above, though built at either end of the sixteenth century. These are known as the Procuratie, from the title of Procurator given to the senior magistrates of Venice, whose residence was formerly in a Byzantine palace on the left side of the square. In 1500 this palace was replaced by the first stage of the present structure, designed by Mauro Coducci (or Codussi as the Venetians like to render his name), an architect from the Val Brembana north of Bergamo, born around 1440. Coducci, whose style plays astonishing variations on early Renaissance themes in a uniquely personal decorative idiom, created some of his most free-ranging designs for

Venetian churches such as San Zaccaria and religious buildings such as the Scuola di San Giovanni Evangelista, though what you see here in the Procuratie Vecchie was continued after his death in 1504 by Bartolomeo Bon (1463–1529) assisted by Guglielmo Grigi.

The pattern established by Coducci's portico was repeated in a loftier, more overweening classical language by Vincenzo Scamozzi (1552–1616) on the opposite side of the square in the Procuratie Nuove, where the line of deeply-incised arches above a raised pavement of pink and yellow marble was completed in 1640 by Baldassare Longhena (1568–1662), the architect of Santa Maria della Salute. This colonnade is more popular with strollers than its earlier counterpart, and the vista under its stuccoed vaulting is one of those many in Venice which has caught the imagination of painters and scene designers.

Halfway down the Procuratie Nuove lies the Cafe Florian, one of the three or four Italian cafes (among them the Greco at Rome and the Pedrocchi at Padua) which the state has designated historic monuments. 'Florian's', as English Venetophiles tend to call it, is an extraordinary survival from the great age of the cafe in the nineteenth century, when such places combined the functions of a restaurant, a reading room, a study and a salon. Its rooms have retained not merely their crimson-upholstered banquettes, chairs and marble-topped tables but also a remarkable series of gaudily-painted glass panels showing women whom a Victorian visitor might well have described as 'no better than they should be', wearing next to nothing and smoking cigars.

The original Florian first opened his cafe here in the eighteenth century, and everyone with any feeling for 'the done thing' in Venice, from Goethe and Rousseau to Henry James and W. H. Auden, has come here to eat an ice, drink a cocktail and listen to the little orchestra, the only one in the square not to make use of amplified sound or to dispense anachronistic theme tunes from movie soundtracks or big numbers from Broadway musicals, instead of the operetta schmaltz and Belle Epoque dance music which really belongs to this sort of band. Florian's always had more taste than its rivals under the Procuratie Vecchie: during the Hapsburg period, true Italian patriots gathered here, shunning the Austrian officers who went over the way to Quadri and Lavena, and whose military band concerts in the Piazza were ostentatiously unapplauded by the native Venetians.

Thomas Adolphus Trollope, brother of the famous novelist and a lifelong resident in Italy, pictured Venetian cafe life for his nineteenth-century readers. 'Some take their evening ice or coffee on the seats under the arcade, and thus have an opportunity of observing the never-ceasing and ever-varying stream of life that flows by them. But the vast majority of the crowd place themselves on chairs arranged around little tables set out on the flags of the piazza. A London or New York policeman would have his very soul revolted, and conclude that there was something very rotten indeed in the state of a city in which the public way could be thus encumbered. Probably, if a Venetian were asked by what right he does so, the question would seem to him much as if one asked by what right the tide covers the shallows of the lagoon. It has always been so, it is in the natural order of things. And how could Venice live without Florian's?'

Should you find yourself at Saint Mark's at a minute or two to the hour, stay where you are, for soon the chimes will be struck in the clocktower at the end of the Procuratie Vecchie by two bronze Moors (or 'wild men' as Thomas Coryate called them) armed with hammers. This Torre dell'Orologio, decorated with painting and gilding, was designed by Mauro Coducci in 1496–99 and augmented during the mid-eighteenth century. The massive clock will tell you not merely the time of day, but the moon's phases and the passage of the sun through the various zodiacal signs.

To the right of the clocktower, directly in front of the Basilica of San Marco, stand three tall masts made of bronze which traditionally carried the banners of the Republic and represented Venice's principal Mediterranean possessions, the islands of Crete and Cyprus, and Euboea, known by its Italian name of Negroponte. You may or may not care for the great flocks of pigeons fluttering and squawking beneath them, but you should at least remember that these are another sacrosanct Venetian institution, even if their guano deposits have had a sad effect on the city's stonework. They are said to have been welcomed and fed here since the days when the crusader Doge Enrico Dandolo used them as message-carriers, though they may simply be descendants of those it was once the custom to release every Palm Sunday.

A pigeon's-eye view of the city, and one of the most exhilarating vistas in the world, suddenly bursts upon the sight as you reach the top of the tremendous Campanile, tallest and always least forgettable of all those belltowers which, for any Italian, symbolize the beloved home town or village. This Campanile, up which you climb in a special lift, is actually a skilful restoration of the original brick shaft, topped with a conical steeple and a golden angel, begun in the ninth century and given its final form in 1515. After centuries of buffeting by wind and thunderstorms, the tower subsided, with the greatest imaginable grace and audible groan, at ten o'clock on the morning of the 14th July, 1902. As luck would have it, nobody was hurt, and what is more, a photographer was on hand to record the spectacular moment of collapse. You can find copies of this remarkable photographic image at various shops throughout central Venice.

From the Campanile the traveller gains a powerful insight into the surrounding urban physiology, its prevailing colours, masses and outlines and the ways whereby it integrates with the scatter of islands across the lagoon. On clear days you can also understand something of its historically ambivalent relationship with the mainland and get a glimpse of that ghostly backdrop of distant, snow-capped Dolomites which provides a blue distance for so many of the classic Venetian painters of the Renaissance and the eighteenth century.

Nowadays the bells inside the tower are seldom rung all together, and some were in any case severely damaged in the fall of 1902. Each had a name and an allotted function: the Trottiera, for example, called the senate to meetings in the Doge's Palace and the Ringhiera tolled for executions. One voice, however, is heard right across the city every midnight, and I know of few more lonely, haunting, special sounds than that of the great Marangona pealing through the shadows of silent *calli* and deserted *campi*, a primal spirit of solitude.

The name 'Marangona' comes from a word meaning 'craftsman', because it was originally rung in the morning as a signal to the various trade guilds to start their work. Few of these skilled labourers can have been more deft in their mystery than those who helped Jacopo Sansovino to create the little Loggetta at the foot of the Campanile. Begun in 1537, this took nearly twelve years to complete, and its elaborate fusion of coloured marbles, composite capitals, sculptured allegories of Venice, Cyprus and Crete, and bronze statues of tutelary deities, as well as the set of wrought metal gates added two centuries later by Antonio Gai (1686–1769), makes it almost too grand for a mere guard-house, which for a long time it was. Almost totally crushed by the falling belltower, the Loggetta has only recently been given a full restoration by the British Venice In Peril Fund, an organization which has done more than most to conserve and reanimate the city's artistic patrimony.

After exalted hubris at the top of a 98-metre-high belfry, you should now be prepared for a little humility, and there is really nothing like the Basilica of San Marco for inducing an entirely genuine feeling of lowliness in the presence of God. If you are not religious, you are still likely to feel humbled by the sheer solemn gorgeousness presented to you in the name of worship, meditation and prayer. You are about to enter one of the great sacred buildings of the world, and though the experience of actually getting inside the church is not an especially uplifting one, accompanied as you almost certainly will be by a suffocating throng of tourists all trying to move at the same time through exceedingly narrow doors, something in the half-light within, the gleam of gold-ground mosaic, a cluster of candles in front of a wonder-working icon, the rippling veins within a marble column, will give you that ideal first intimation of 'something rich and strange', the richest and strangest thing perhaps in all Venice.

Saint Mark's starts catching you by the throat before you have even set foot inside it. The building's unique nature, as a symbol of Venice's achievement in freeing itself from the threat of foreign overlordship and in acquiring status and dignity among the cities of Christendom in the possession of a martyred Evangelist, is made apparent by the wonderfully unashamed assertiveness of the façade, hitting the astonished eye as the traveller emerges into the full daylight of the Piazza.

Venice shelters the bodies of several saints, nearly all of them looted from Byzantine churches in the course of imperial conquest, and the bones of Saint Mark constitute the most spectacular sanctified booty of them all. Until the beginning of the ninth century, the Republic's patron was Saint Theodore – 'San Todaro' as the Venetians call him – a perfectly respectable Greek holy man, but hardly in the same order as the earliest of the gospel-writers. In the year 828 two merchants, Buono di Malamocco and Rustico da Torcello, while on a voyage to Alexandria, managed to persuade the monks of a certain monastery sheltering Saint Mark's body that the evangelist should be placed out of reach of desecration by the Muslim rulers of Egypt. With a cunning typically Venetian, they smuggled the bones away by wrapping them in pork and calling out in Arabic 'Kanzir! Kanzir!', 'Pig! Pig!' as they passed through the streets, so as to deter pious Mohammedans from too close an inspection. Getting their precious burden on deck, they tied it to the mainmast and a miraculous intervention by the saint saved the ship from wreck on its homeward voyage through a terrible storm. The body was housed within a shrine enclosed by a basilica, and a legend, presumably devised to authenticate the saint's enforced translation, told how he had once halted on an island in the lagoon, where an angel had appeared, prophesying to him that he would at length find a resting place among the Venetians. Hereafter the Republic adopted the Evangelist's symbol of a winged lion bearing the angelic greeting 'Pax tibi Marce Evangelista meus', 'Peace be unto you, Mark my Evangelist'.

Nothing survives of the earliest church dedicated to him, or of its successor, except possibly the original ground plan. Neither was intended as a cathedral. Until 1807, that honour belonged to the church of San Pietro in Castello, at the city's eastern edge, and the present building, begun during the reign of Doge Domenico Contarini (1043–1071) was raised as a basilica, along the lines of such churches as the Lateran in Rome or Sant'Ambrogio at Milan. Its purpose was to fulfil the functions of a palatine chapel, in which the grandest rituals of the state, symbolized by the Doge whose palace stood nearby, could be fittingly carried out.

Though it is believed the craftsmen from Lombardy and Florence must have contributed to adorning the new church of Saint Mark, its design and overall character are self-consciously Greek. The architects, whose names are not yet known to us (though amid the vast impacted mass of Venetian documents their identity perhaps lies buried), were probably Byzantine, and

27

the presence of brick domes and mosaic ceiling and wall decorations were decided indicators that Venice looked east rather than west for its political involvements in the early Middle Ages, just as the extensive use of sculptured marble on the exterior walls formed an obvious allusion to that ancient Rome which the Serene Republic wished the world to accept as her immediate ancestor.

Marbles and mosaics and the curve of domed roofs form dominant themes in the music of the façade, as indeed does the building's only significant Gothic element, the beautiful sequence of crocketed canopies and tall pinnacled aedicules above the round-headed arches of its lower storey. Ruskin, whose prose is an eternally thrilled, and thrilling, response to the impact of Venice on a northern European sensitivity rooted in Calvinism and starved of visual enchantment, tells us how 'the crests of the arches break into a marble foam, and toss themselves far into the blue sky in flashes and wreaths of sculptured spray, as if the breakers on the Lido shore had been frostbound before they fell, and the sea nymphs had inlaid them with coral and amethyst'. Remember these images, for you will certainly come across more of this idiosyncratic late mediaeval stone carving in your walks through Venice, and the marine inspirations behind Venetian Gothic have never been more ecstatically captured in words.

What sealed the basilica's destiny as the religious treasurehouse of the Republic was its adornment, in the early thirteenth century, with some of those splendid things brought back by the merchant captains who so opportunely took the crusaders to raid Constantinople in 1204. 'Old blind Dandolo' the doughty doge did not return (you will find his simple gravestone in one of the galleries of the church of Agia Sophia in modern Istanbul) but his followers were careful to carry away the most gorgeous carvings, gemstones, gold and statuary with them, to make San Marco into an incontrovertible statement of majesty and power, temporal as well as spiritual.

Several of these trophies, brought not only from Constantinople but from other eastern cities such as Acre, decorate the north side of the church, in the form of panels of carved marble. Another spoil of conquest is the sculpted porphyry ensemble of four cloaked figures embracing one another, set as a kind of eyecatcher on the southwestern corner of the basilica. The diadems they wear emphasize a royal status, and they are indeed the Roman Emperor Diocletian (285–303) and his three imperial co-rulers, Maximilian, Constantius and Galerius.

Nothing could better underline Venice's desire to re-enact the experience of the Roman Empire, though Dandolo and his fellow raiders may not actually have known the identity of their distinguished stone effigies. Nothing, that is, save the most famous Byzantine booty of all, whose presence on the church's façade was seen by envious foreign powers as a kind of perpetual taunt at all those who dreamed of humbling the pride of La Serenissima. The four bronze 'horses of Saint Mark' are thought originally to have been made in Greece to adorn a Roman palace, but were at length used to decorate the Hippodrome of Constantinople, the chariot racecourse notorious for its factional strife between 'blues' and 'greens' during the reign of Justinian and Theodora in the sixth century.

Much has been written about these animals, both as magnificent artefacts and as a guide to the kind of horses bred and ridden in the ancient world. Goethe, for instance, hailed them as 'a glorious team – I should like to hear the opinion of a good judge of horseflesh. What seemed strange to me was that, viewed closely they appear heavy, while from the Piazza below they look as light as deer.' That wonderfully disenchanted eighteenth-century French traveller in Italy, the President de Brosses, considered them 'the only things throughout the whole building worthy of admiration'. The French indeed, during the Napoleonic occupation of the city, took them all the way to Paris, and it was with a very bad grace that they gave them up in 1815, when the whirligig of fate sent Napoleon to St Helena and the Byzantine loot was returned to its original looters.

Once inside Saint Mark's the visitor surrenders at once to its atmosphere of richly-charged mystery. The effect, as you stand in the central space – it always seems much wider than an ordinary mediaeval nave and more like the atrium of a Roman bath-house – is like being inside a body, with bones of brick covered with skin and tissue of marble and mosaic. You feel that the very stone will glow warm to your touch, and that the veins running through it are real blood vessels. A patina of extreme old age lies across everything, embodied best of all by the floor's undulating surface, with its hillocks and hollows like those of a sand dune.

Among the most venerable of the church's Byzantine decorative features are the patches of twelfth-century mosaic work, though most of the Saint Mark's mosaics belong to the thirteenth century, and many were later restored. Several of the themes and specific locations in the overall scheme will be familiar to anyone who has entered a Greek church. In the concave of the apse, for example, is a looming Christ Pantocrator, and in the central cupola is an Ascension scene. Elsewhere, the sequences concentrate on individual saints, several of them more popular in the Orthodox than in the Roman calendar, emphasizing Venice's eastward orientation. My personal favourite among them all is the enchantingly busy, colourful series decorating the chapel on the corner of the north transept, illustrating the story of Saint Isidore and the translation of his body to Venice. Isidore's was another set of stolen bones, lifted from the island of Chios (where his name is still favoured at baptism) by Doge Domenico Michiel in 1125, and hidden for two hundred years in case the Greeks dared to ask for it back. These vital, intensely-imagined episodes from Isidore's story were executed in the mid-fourteenth century at the order of Doge Andrea Dandolo (1342–1354), a scholarly patrician who befriended the poet Petrarch. Dandolo also commissioned a fine tomb sculpture of the recumbent saint, visited by an angel, with two scenes from his martyrdom (he was tied to the tail of a wild horse and then beheaded). Just outside the chapel, under a canopy, is one of several wonderworking Byzantine Madonnas brought to Venice from Constantinople. This one, called Nikopeia, Bringer of Victory, is a tenth-century icon set in a splendid frame of silver and enamel.

But what of Saint Mark himself, the principal object of our veneration? His relics lie under the high altar, separated from the body of the church by an iconostasis in the form of a screen topped with marble statues of the Apostles, carved by Jacobello and Pierpaolo delle Masegne in 1394. The altar itself was once adorned with a frontal of gold and precious stones, known as the Pala d'Oro, which has now been placed behind it for closer inspection. Incorporating work from earlier frontals belonging to the tenth and eleventh centuries, the Pala d'Oro received its present form during the mid-fourteenth century, when the Gothic framework was designed to surround a rich cluster of jewels, enamels and carvings. Derived in part from the spoils of 1204, the two tiers of the altarpiece show the Archangel Michael amid saints and New Testament figures, and below this a Christ Panto-crator flanked by scenes from the lives of the four Evangelists.

As Augustus Hare rightly observed in his Victorian guidebook to Venice, 'it is the general impression, not the detail, of Saint Mark's which makes it so transcendent'. You can admire the individual beauties of a mosaic ceiling, or a Doge's tomb such as that of Andrea Dandolo in the Baptistery, or Sansovino's finely wrought bronze sacristy doors of 1546, let alone the extraordinary scatter of silver and gold, polished alabaster and crystal, which fills the basilica's treasury, but in the end it is the total impact of these things, working together on the dazzled senses, which will lure you back again and again into the consecrated darkness of the church. Blasé as you may grow during successive visits to Venice, you and Saint Mark will never have done with one another.

When you step out once more into the Piazza, it is only natural that you should rub your eyes a little dizzily as the daylight hits you again, but look down at the simple red and white marble lozenge in the floor of the atrium below the steps of the main door. It was here, on 24th July 1177, that the Holy Roman Emperor Frederick Barbarossa, whose arrogance had driven him to defy the Papacy for almost twenty years, was reconciled to Pope Alexander III in the presence of the Doge and the senators.

Before the papal throne Frederick doffed his crimson mantle, prostrating himself on the pavement, then kissing the pontiff's feet and embracing his knees. Moved to tears, the victorious Alexander returned the embrace, though he rebuffed the Emperor's last defiant words *'Non tibi sed Petro'* – 'Not to you but to Saint Peter' – with a firm *'Et mihi et Petro'*, 'Both to me and Saint Peter', before the pair entered the church to hear a Te Deum. According to the chroniclers, Alexander sealed his triumph by sending Barbarossa a fatted calf to eat, with the appropriate quotation from the parable of the Prodigal Son who 'was lost and is found'.

Next to the basilica stands the Doge's Palace, whose long spans of Gothic arcading, forming a double loggia underneath an upper storey of diamond-patterned pink and white brick, were begun in 1340 by an architect named Piero Baseio and continued in 1424 after a fire destroyed part of the building. Further fires during the next hundred years demanded more restoration, but the outer shell of the palace has always retained its late mediaeval form, despite changes in style reflected in the surrounding architecture. Seen in this context, the great works of Piazza San Marco, the basilica, the porticoes, Sansovino's library and the palace itself form a magnificent riposte to our modern obsession with building 'in keeping'. None of these edifices is in keeping with the others, but their self-confidence is such that we willingly accept them as part of one of the world's grandest architectural complexes.

So it is with the Doge's Palace. Assertiveness is the keynote here, proclaiming the inflexible certainties of Venetian republican government, whose bureaucratic control over an empire stemmed from the various departments of state which had their offices here. In the palace the senate and various councils met, the lawyers prepared their cases and the notaries drew up documents, sailors were recruited for battleships of the fleet, and the Doge received the embassies of foreign powers.

You enter the central courtyard through the Porta della Carta, an exuberant essay in mature Venetian Gothic, built between 1438 and 1442 by the brothers Bartolomeo and Giovanni Bon (the former's signature is cut into the architrave). Under the window, with its small quatrefoil lights above, flanked by allegories of the virtues in little tabernacles, Doge Francesco Foscari kneels before the Lion of Saint Mark. Foscari was one of the most forceful of all the doges, whose long reign, beginning in 1423, saw Venice reaching its zenith of power and influence, but in 1457 he was compelled to abdicate, owing to the trial of his son Jacopo for murder. The accusation was never proved, though Jacopo was exiled to Crete, and it was always believed that the whole episode had been cunningly set up by members of the Loredan family, bearers of a longstanding grudge against the Foscari. The double shame hastened Francesco's death, and four centuries afterwards his sad story was turned into a highly effective verse drama by Lord Byron, *The Two Foscari*, out of which Giuseppe Verdi made one of his early operas.

Inside the courtyard the architectural perspectives become increasingly theatrical. The earliest portion is the colonnade and loggia immediately facing you, begun in 1483 by Antonio Rizzo, who died in 1498, when the work was taken over by the more assured hand of Pietro Lombardo (1435–1515). The southern and western portions are a sympathetic continuation of the original rhythm by the early seventeenth-century architect Bartolomeo Monopola. On the side closest to Saint Mark's, enclosing the so-called Courtyard of the Senators, stands a pretty little Renaissance pavilion which was once the Doge's private chapel, dedicated to Saint Nicholas, and next to this is Rizzo's masterstroke, the Scala dei Giganti, a lavishly-adorned marble staircase guarded by two larger-than-life statues of Mercury and Neptune, tutelary gods of merchants and the sea, carved by Jacopo Sansovino in 1566.

These stairs are the cause of a notorious literary howler, in another of Byron's Venetian dramas, *Marino Faliero*, based on the downfall of the unlucky Doge Marin Falier, who took office in 1354 at the age of seventy-six. From the very start of his brief reign he was beset by misfortune. On the day when he should have landed in ceremonious triumph from the Bucintoro, the

33

Republic's great barge of state, the lagoon was swathed in one of its notorious autumnal fogs, so he had to be put ashore from a humble rowing boat called a *piatta*. At his inaugural banquet, a roistering young nobleman started making indecent passes at one of the Dogaressa's ladies-in-waiting, and left a ribald message on Falier's throne before being flung out of the palace.

Incensed by the insolent licence of the youthful nobles in general, Falier decided to take the whole patrician class (his own, be it noted) in hand by staging a coup designed to make him despot of Venice. The Council of Ten got wind of it in time, most of the conspirators were hanged, and the Doge himself was beheaded at the top of the courtyard staircase – too early for the famous curtain line of Byron's play:

'The gory head rolls down the Giants' Steps'

to which the answer is that in 1355 of course it couldn't have, but the Scala dei Giganti always invites you to imagine it.

You generally enter the palace by another staircase altogether, either the Scala dei Censori in the northeast corner, or the fantastically stuccoed Scala d'Oro, whose ceiling decorations are by the greatest sixteenth-century Venetian sculptor Alessandro Vittoria (1524–1608), an apprentice in Sansovino's workshop. Henceforward the sequence ensues of grand halls and saloons for the various councils, for the reception of ambassadors and for the public presentation of the Doge as the figurehead of state. It has to be said that the Doge's Palace, however palatial, is curiously lacking in any of that lived-in feeling which even the most provincial-looking staterooms of some petty prince or tenth-rate duke always manage to convey. Naturally this has something to do with its insensitive and humiliating conversion, by the Austrians in the nineteenth century, into government offices, but it owes more than a little to the whole nature of the Venetian political framework, which resulted in a building very different in character from an opulent family residence for a ruling dynasty.

Alas, there is no space in which to lead you systematically from room to room (many are now used as exhibition spaces) but a word or two should be said about the finest of them, since the palace as we now have it is a showcase for some of the boldest, most ambitious artistic achievements of the late sixteenth century.

Two artists in particular stand out here, though each is encountered in a more intensely personal, less markedly official guise elsewhere in the city. Jacopo Robusti, known by his nickname of Tintoretto (1518–1594), 'the little dyer', spent nearly all his life in Venice as an amazingly versatile and productive painter, specializing in portraits and religious scenes reflecting his devout Christian piety. His most grandiose achievement is the enormous vision of Paradise filling the end wall of the Sala del Maggior Consiglio, which housed the thousand-strong assembly of nobles forming the governing elite and was also used for welcoming foreign princes and potentates.

As a backdrop to the Doge's throne, Tintoretto's massive painting, completed in 1590 and intended to replace a similar work destroyed in the fifteenth-century fire, represents both an ardent realization of Dante's poetic Paradise and, through its key position in this political theatre of republican Venice, an obvious hint to the bedazzled onlooker that after such a perfection of state government the next stop can only be Heaven itself. It is in any case an extraordinary synthesis of swirling, diving, dancing hierarchies of angels, saints, prophets and evangelists, beatific in their perpetual glorification of Christ and the Blessed Virgin.

The notion of Venice as an exalted abstract, a concept personified to form the dominant motif in a decorative scheme, inspired Tintoretto's most gifted contemporary, Paolo Caliari, known as Veronese (1530–1588) from his birthplace at Verona. His was a far less sombre and self-consciously dramatic imagination than Tintoretto's, and his palette, with its prodigal colour range, through jade green and deep yellow ochre to rich crimson and luminous blue, is the most varied of any Venetian painter between Titian (1488–1576) and Tiepolo (1696–1770). In his role as a painter for doges and senators Veronese is best seen in the Sala del Collegio, the splendid hall designed by Andrea Palladio

(1508–1580) for the ducal reception of magistrates and returning ambassadors, as well as the representatives of foreign powers accredited to the Republic. The lavishly gilded ceiling frames a sequence of allegories, the calm-eyed Serenissima herself, ministered to by Peace and Justice, Fidelity accompanied by a dog, Meekness stroking a lamb, Moderation pulling a feather from an eagle's wing, which illustrate Veronese's unique gift for imbuing his most lyrical fancies with a numinous solemnity. On the wall above the dais where the Doge and his council sat is a further Veronesian masterstroke, an epiphany of the Redeemer, Saint Mark and Saint Justina, with Doge Sebastiano Venier kneeling before them in thanks for the great victory of Lepanto on 7th October 1571, when the allied fleets of Venice and Spain defeated the Turks in a tremendous sea fight off the Peloponnesian coast.

The theme of victorious Venice is carried triumphantly, by Tintoretto and Veronese, with their pupils and followers, across the walls and ceilings of the palace, underlining the success of the Venetian government on the level of image-making and public relations, let alone on any other more practical basis. That the palace was first and foremost an administrative centre is nevertheless emphasized by the names of the various rooms, the Sala dello Scrutinio, where electoral votes were scrutinized, the Sala della Quarantia, where an appeal court of forty councillors examined civil cases, or the Retrostanza dei Capi, where three chief inquisitors sat in a little leather-lined study to examine those accused of high crimes against the state.

Inevitably this last apartment had a small torture chamber above it, from which a passage led to the so-called Ponte dei Sospiri, the Bridge of Sighs, thence into the prisons on the other side of a small canal. The bridge, an elegant little confection by the Swiss-born architect Antonio di Bernardino Contino (1566–1600), probably did hear a sigh or two, though these were likely to come from hard-pressed palace bureaucrats, since only one political prisoner ever crossed it. The awfulness of the ducal prisons, in comparison with those to be found elsewhere in early modern Europe, has been hugely exaggerated. Known as *pozzi*,

37

wells, the lower cells look suitably dismal, covered as their walls are with the marks of candle smoke and traces of old graffiti, but they were clean and well ventilated enough for the purpose of confining the petty criminals assigned to them. From another more comfortable set of cells in the roof of the palace itself, called the *piombi*, leads, that most glamorous and garrulous of eighteenth-century bounders, Casanova, or, to give him his full name, Giacomo Casanova di Seingalt, made a dramatic escape in 1756, ending a not especially dreary term of imprisonment by walking unscathed out of the palace, hopping into a gondola and taking a leisurely ride to the mainland. Only under the Austrians were political detainees kept here, including the writer Silvio Pellico, whose *I miei prigioni (My Prisons)* is one of the greatest of all captivity memoirs, and the lawyer Daniele Manin who so gallantly led the 1848–9 revolt.

You will find a fascinating survival of the anti-Austrian revolution on the last pillar of the colonnade facing you as you emerge from the Doge's Palace into the Piazzetta, the little square opening off the main Piazza San Marco onto the lagoon. Barely discernible, yet still visibly there under the grimy patina of a century and a half, are the words 'Viva La Repubblica, Viva San Marco' stencilled onto the stonework by a patriotic hand.

The two tall free-standing columns facing you as you gaze towards the water were originally brought from the eastern Mediterranean and set up here in 1172. Atop the left-hand pillar crouches the Lion of Saint Mark, a bronze image which began life as an antique chimera before being adapted to its present purpose. On the companion monolith stands the figure of Saint Theodore, his co-patron, scrambled together from various Hellenistic bits and accompanied by what looks like a crocodile but is actually a dragon.

The colonnade forms part of Jacopo Sansovino's nobly conceived library building, begun in 1537 to house the Biblioteca Marciana, the state collection of codices, books and manuscripts, whose nucleus was created from collections by the poet Petrarch and by the remarkable Johannes Bessarion (1396–1472), a Greek monk from Trebizond who converted to Catholicism and was made a cardinal and Bishop of Frascati, near Rome. The lines of Doric and Ionic columns along the lower and upper storeys, the elegant garlands around the windows and the crowning parapet with its obelisks and mythologies made Sansovino's library one of the most dramatically influential works of its time, and echoes of its impact can be felt all over Venice and such mainland satellite cities as Verona and Bergamo. No wonder Andrea Palladio called it 'the most richly adorned building that ever was made, from ancient times until the present day', though the cafes below and the giant banner advertisements for current exhibitions are not exactly helpful to the appreciative eye.

The gilded hall on the first floor, where the library's richest treasures were formerly displayed, has long been closed to public view, but should you feel studiously inquisitive as to matters Venetian, the Biblioteca Marciana will welcome you to its noisy reading room, to its idiosyncratic cataloguing system and not always especially cooperative staff, and to a wealth of Byzantine manuscripts, classical editions from the press of Aldus Manutius established at Venice in 1492, and early musical scores, including the fascinating Contarini archive of seventeenth-century operas from the age of Monteverdi and Cavalli.

Outside the library door, flanked by two burly stone atlanti, turn left, passing the Archaeological Museum, always closed but housing a collection of antique sculpture on which sixteenth-century painters based many of their poses and groupings. Once in the Piazza, assuming you may have stopped for a drink at Florian's, follow the arcade into the main portico and climb the monumental stairs leading to the Ala Napoleonica.

This, together with the adjoining upper storeys of the Procuratie Nuove, now houses the Correr Museum, a place which manages to scoop up into its various galleries and showcases most of the history of Venice from the Middle Ages to the nineteenth century. Teodoro Correr was one of several patricians who, after the Hapsburg imperial takeover of the fallen Republic became a *fait accompli*, seem to have ended up as the last representatives of their distinguished lines. In certain cases this simply meant selling off their palaces and heirlooms to affluent foreigners, but Correr left his property, including an art collection, to the city, and this provided the basis for a display of Venetian life laying special emphasis on the paraphernalia of state ceremonial.

Thus the atmosphere in the Correr is a bit like being backstage at a theatre, with the various props and costumes from some lavish spectacle you have just missed but whose character is still unmistakably vivid. Here are the robes of senators and councillors in pink and crimson satin and brocade, here are the little ivory *ballotti* used in ducal elections, here is a *bocca di leone*, one of the sinister stone letter boxes carved in the form of a lion's mouth, for the reception of secret denunciations. One room holds a complete set of stately Baroque monastic bookcases, another flourishes banners captured from Turkish galleys, and yet another displays the various coins and medals of the state, including the silver medallions distributed to patricians by the Doge at his enthronement. These were called *oselle*, little birds, because originally the tokens came in the form of five ducks killed on the marshes of the lagoon, though eventually the breeding habits of the nobility proved too much for the local birdlife to keep up with, and roundels of silver were handed out instead.

On the floor above, a picture gallery displays the somewhat tentative evolution of a Gothic style in Venetian painting, but much more interest develops when we come to Antonello da Messina, Giovanni Bellini and Alvise Vivarini, all of whom felt the influence of fifteenth-century Flemish painters whose art had been introduced to Venice through trade with cities such as Antwerp, Bruges and Ghent. Augustus Hare, writing when the Correr Museum was housed in the Fondaco dei Turchi on the Grand Canal, snootily dismissed the pictures as 'mostly indifferent', describing one of them as 'exorbitantly extolled by Ruskin'. This was the famous painting of two women sitting on a housetop with their dogs, part of a larger work, now lost, by Vettor Carpaccio (1486–1525). Nobody is quite sure whether the figures are those of Venetian courtesans, of which the city was rumoured to contain several thousand, or respectable merchants' wives, but where the picture itself is concerned, Ruskin's enthusiasm, as so often, was perfectly judged.

From the Correr Museum, you leave the Piazza behind, to follow the Salizzada San Moise, which forms the beginning of what is essentially a long shopping street interrupted by bridges, churches and canals, stretching as far as the Campo Stefano. Down the Calle Vallaresso, at the first left turn, is the little Teatro del Ridotto, a theatre made out of an elegantly appointed eighteenth-century gambling saloon. Georgian Londoners got hold of the name 'Ridotto' and applied it to any sort of fashionable assembly. Nowadays those in search of Venetian smartness may find some of it at Harry's Bar across the way, the fruit of American expatriate yearning, between the world wars, for a decent drinking hole.

Back in the Salizzada (a term meaning a brick-paved street) you reach the side entrance of San Moise, but pass on to the front of the church, so as to relish the visual bizarrerie of its façade. Ruskin called this astonishing scramble of allegories and camels and palm trees and geological whatnots 'one of the basest examples of the basest school of the Renaissance', and it was hardly a triumph for either the architect Alessandro Tremignon or the sculptor Heinrich Meyring (dates for each unknown) who raised it in 1668, fulfilling the terms of a bequest from a johnny-come-lately patrician Vincenzo Fini. Yes, it is vulgar, clumsy, ill-managed, not even successful as a morsel of high camp, yet so much has it become a part of the Venetian scene that I should be sorry to see it go.

Inside, the darkness falls so thickly that it is hard to see some of the more than merely passable late Baroque and Rococo painting and sculpture, but don't miss the expressive marble Pieta above the altar, by Antonio Corradini (1668–1752), a sculptor from the little town of Este and near Padua, or the bright-toned panels of the organ case, by Francesco Migliori (1684–1734) and Francesco Pittoni, uncle of the more famous Giambattista (1687–1767) who made such a name as a painter of fantasy ruins and monumental interiors. A simple inscription on a stone in the floor at the centre of the church marks the grave of John Law, who died in 1729 after a sensational career as an international fraudster and wheeler-dealer, floating companies with nonexistent assets which attracted runaway investors of a most desirable kind. A Scot who took refuge in France after killing his opponent in a duel, he created the French equivalent of the English South Sea Bubble with his Mississippi scheme, and went on with his grand scams even after fleeing to Venice in 1720.

Outside the church, whose aged mediaeval campanile stands somewhat behind it to the right, is the Hotel Bauer Grunwald, which, as one of central Venice's few modern buildings, has attracted more attention than its boring façade really justifies. Cross the bridge and walk along the broad Calle XXII Marzo, commemorating the day when the Austrians were chased out of Venice in 1848. The street's width, as well as the name, tells you that it is comparatively new, dating from the late nineteenth century. At the end, turn left, then right, crossing the next canal (on the other side of the bridge some local animal-lover regularly puts out a pail full of water for thirty dogs), and this will bring you into the broad *campo* in front of Santa Maria del Giglio.

This church is also known as Santa Maria Zobenigo, after the extinct Jubanico family who founded it in the ninth century (the funny little brick blockhouse in the *campo* is all that remains of the belltower). What we now see is essentially a Baroque building, whose most arresting external feature is the extravagant façade tacked onto its northern end between 1678 and 1683, and commissioned by members of the Barbaro family who lived nearby.

I have to confess that this is one of my Venetian favourites, though my taste is unlikely to be shared by very many readers, since those who can stomach the arch-theatricality of baroque art are comparatively few. The whole ensemble, designed by Giuseppe Sardi (d. 1699), celebrates unashamedly the greater glory of the Barbaro, and here they are, posing in their splendid curlings periwigs, as senators, procurators, admirals and generals, framed by female allegories, above a sequence of little relief maps of the cities and islands they governed, Zara, Crete, Padua, Rome, Corfu and Split. The work was intended as a perpetual fling at Doge Francesco Morosini, heroic commander of Venetian armies in the Pelopponese, who had sacked Antonio Barbaro for military incompetence. We must hope that some cultural rescue fund soon has the wit to clean it, though the layers of accumulated pigeon-droppings over the periwigs seem fortuitously decorative.

Inside, the church has an appealing brightness occasioned by a profusion of white stucco on walls and ceilings. An enchanting feature is the statuary group of the Annunciation on the high altar, with the humble Virgin – 'behold the handmaid of the Lord' – on one side and the kneeling Angel – 'hail Mary, thou that art highly favoured' – on the other, seventeenth-century work by Heinrich Meyring. There is a fine barbaric-sounding old organ on which recitals are often given, but its doors, painted by Tintoretto with sturdy figures of the Four Evangelists, have been brought down to be displayed below. The sacristy glitters with silver reliquaries showing gruesome specimens of saintly bone, hair, teeth, nails, each with authenticating labels. Probably not so authentic, alas, is the so-called Rubens, a Madonna and Child in very bad condition.

At the end of the *campo*, beyond the Gritti Palace Hotel, is the *traghetto* which takes you over to the Salute. As an alternative expedition, however, turn left, walk past the Barbaro façade and through the archway, leading you out along a secluded canal and over a bridge. This offers a glimpse of the glass-canopied water-gate to the Fenice Theatre, where on occasional gala evenings Very Important People arrive by gondola. Walk under the little arcade and turn up the alley past the stage door. This will bring you out into the Campo San Fantin, to look up at the theatre's colonnaded façade.

The Gran Teatro della Fenice was completed in 1792 by Antonio Selva (1757–1819), a highly intelligent, well-travelled architect (he visited England and made a careful study of landscape gardens) whose design was not greatly liked by the

Venetians. They chose to interpret the letters of the word 'Socie-tas' above the portico as standing for '*Sine ordine cum irregularitate erexit theatrum Antonius Selva*'. Phoenix – Fenice – indeed the theatre was rebuilt after a serious fire in 1836, but the chaste elegance of Selva's interior was largely retained, and the cream and gold auditorium, with its gorgeous ducal box dominating rows of pink-upholstered stalls, is surely the loveliest in Italy, one of those theatres which lift the heart in excited anticipation as soon as you set foot in its marble foyer.

The first opera given here was *I giochi di Agrigento*, by Giovanni Paisiello (1740–1816), a Neapolitan who was Napoleon Bona-parte's favourite composer. During the nineteenth century the Fenice was one of the three or four major opera houses of Italy, and such great masters as Donizetti and Bellini scored signal triumphs here, but its most famous associations are with the work of Giuseppe Verdi. Two of his most successful early operas, *Ernani* (1844) and *Attila* (1846), won instant acclaim here, and *Rigoletto* (1851) scored an immediate hit. Surprisingly *La Traviata*, given two years later, failed to make an impact, owing, some said, to the implausibly buxom soprano Fanny Salvini-Donatelli in the role of the consumptive Violetta. After the poor reception of *Simon Boccanegra* in 1857, the composer turned his back on La Fenice, though he had good reason to be grateful to its enlight-ened management.

Turning a modern back on the theatre, you confront an attrac-tive architectural ensemble, formed by the church of San Fantin (unremarkable except for its fine apse by Sansovino (1562) and a pleasing painting by the south German artist Josef Heinz (1625–1698) showing the parish priest pleading with the Virgin and saints to save Venice from the plague), the mediaeval Casa Molin with its covered staircase to your right, and the Ateneo Veneto, a literary club housed in what was formerly the Scuola di San Fantin. This charitable institution once sheltered another *scuola*, dedicated to Saint Jerome, whose members, dressed in black hoods, accompanied criminals to execution. On fine eve-nings the theatre crowd spills out into the *campo* during the interval, and after the performance, in time-honoured Venetian style, hangs around in its finery for a gossip (local dialect uses a plural word *ciaccole*, 'chit-chats', with the 'l' sounded like a 'w').

From La Fenice, walk back down the alley past the stage door and turn right, passing the august restaurant where the singers will adjourn for dinner and a wall inset with Austrian guns and cannonballs from the 1848 siege. Crossing under the *sottoportego* (a covered entry) follow the narrow lane which brings you out into the vast, empty space of the Campo Sant'Angelo. Apart from open-air movie shows forming part of the September Venice Film Festival, nothing ever seems to go on here, and late at night the howling loneliness of the place can often seem quite frightening, yet, without really knowing why, I always retain a certain fondness for it. The church of Sant'Angelo (the angel in question was Michael) was demolished in 1837, and the only religious building left is the nondescript mediaeval oratory close by the canal, but the *campo* contains a handful of interesting palaces. In the fifteenth-century Palazzo Duodo (on your left as you come from La Fenice), its pale brickwork punctuated by a sequence of graceful ogival windows, died the Neapolitan composer Domenico Cimarosa (1749–1801). More popular than Mozart in his day, he possessed an inexhaustible talent for comic opera, and recent revivals of his best works, such as *Il matrimonio segreto* and *Le astuzie femminili*, show how much Mozart himself owed to the Italian master's musical wit, charm and sensitivity.

Cross the *campo*, go over the bridge, and you find yourself in front of San Stefano, surely the most beautiful Gothic church in Venice for the uncluttered lightness of its spacious interior and crammed with arresting detail from every age of Venetian art. Originally attached to an Augustinian monastery, suppressed during the Napoleonic period, it was begun in 1294 and finished in 1325, but the portal by which you enter was added in the first half of the fifteenth century. The ornament of the door frame and the delicate fronds curling upwards around the arch between tall pinnacles suggest that this is probably the work of the great

Bartolomeo Bon, already encountered at the Porta della Carta of the Doge's Palace.

What visitors to San Stefano have always admired is the great barrel-vaulted roof over the nave, its triple curves crisscrossed by spars to create the effect of an upturned ship's hull. The inner surfaces are adorned with little painted rosettes, while the beams themselves are likewise covered with floral motifs echoed in the decoration of the larger timbers spanning the two arcades. Each of the arches, what is more, has a surrounding frieze which repeats the foliage pattern of the stonework around the entrance door. Above them are figures of saintly monastic exemplars, Saint Nicholas of Tolentino, Saint Monica, the Blessed Christopher of Piedmont and others, including, of course, Saint Augustine himself.

Along the aisles runs an imposing series of late Baroque marble altars, featuring several accomplished early eighteenth-century altarpieces, a sort of sample catalogue of period taste. The best are surely the restless *Saint Augustine destroying Heresy* by Giustino Menescardi in the right aisle and, on the left, Girolamo Brusaferro's *Saint Mark with the Virgin and Saints* (1732) which has a fully-rigged Venetian galley in the background, as a sign of its commission by the Scuola dei Calafati, the guild of dockyard workers at the Arsenal.

The high altar is a pompous affair of 1656, but on the side walls of the presbytery dignified Renaissance marble panels frame saints in niches. San Stefano keeps its greatest treasures, however, in the sacristy, entered through a door at the end of the right aisle. Here is a trio of magnificent Tintorettos, a Last Supper composed in an arrangement of plunging diagonals, a powerfully evoked Washing of the Feet and a dreamlike Agony in the Garden. The Greek icon below was brought from Nafplion in 1541 by a member of the Barbaro family, and includes, in the silverwork surrounding the faces of the Virgin and Child, the figure of John Cantacuzeno, son of a fourteenth-century despot of Mistra in the Peloponnese. Apart from two brilliant fragments from a lost altarpiece by Bartolomeo Vivarini, the most unashamedly decorative element here is the romantically-conceived series of episodes from the childhood of Christ, complete with a Massacre of the Innocents among Roman ruins and a very Venetian-looking angel boatman preparing to ferry the Holy Family to Egypt. The artist was Gaspare Diziani, who, like so many of his fellows, came down from the Alps to seek his fortune in Venice.

Outside the church the perennially busy Campo San Stefano offers a potent contrast to the deserted Campo Sant'Angelo nearby. At the end closest to the Accademia Bridge stands the seventeenth-century church of San Vidal, now used as an art gallery, to whose left a *fondamenta* (paved canal bank) runs down to the back gate of Palazzo Barbaro, where the novelist Henry James used to stay during the 1880s and 1890s as a guest of its owners the Curtis family, fellow Americans whose drawing room on the *piano nobile* was a gathering place for all the most interesting foreign birds-of-passage in *fin de siècle* Venice. Nearer to you on the right is the strangely low-pitched Renaissance

Palazzo Loredan, over whose doorway you can still faintly trace a German inscription which tells you that this was once used as a garrison for Austrian troops. Appropriately enough, the statue of poet and patriot Niccolo Tommaseo, one of the leaders of the 1848 revolution, has his back turned to it. Generally carrying a pigeon or a seagull on top of his head, he presides benignly over the life of the square, much of which concentrates just outside the church of San Stefano at Cafe Paolin, at whose congenial tables, over your *bitter campari*, your *spremuta di lemone* or your *ombra di vino*, it seems entirely fitting to close this chapter.

3 : In Cannaregio

Tradition always has it that Venice is the most godly city in Italy. Whether this is true or not is impossible to say, but the plethora of churches, nearly all of them still fulfilling their appointed functions, rather suggests that it might be. The situation here recalls John Betjeman's evocation of mediaeval London 'with a tinkling mass-house in every cavernous street', and the traveller in Venice soon learns to speak of journeys, directions and locations in terms of a whole calendar of saints and their parishes.

Once upon a time there were a great many more. After the fall of the Republic in 1797, entire convents and monasteries were swept away, and throughout the nineteenth century some fifty churches were either closed or demolished altogether. Certain parts of Venice positively echo with this ghostly presence of a vanished religious life, and one such area is unquestionably the rather gloomy zone which lies between Campo Sant'Angelo and the Rialto.

In this quarter you are lucky to come across anything of much artistic or historical interest, but here and there among the dead parishes, the long-abandoned *scuole* and the eternally locked surviving churches, there are unexpected eye-catchers in the most unpromising of settings. One of these curiosities is reached by taking the first left turn off the Calle della Mandorla, which leads northwards out of Campo Sant'Angelo, and following it as far as the gateway to the fifteenth-century Gothic Palazzo Pesaro degli Orfei, one of several palaces whose main entrance is up a flight of external stairs to an arcaded loggia.

This was once the home of Mariano Fortuny y Madrazo (1871–1950), a Spanish painter from Granada, whose somewhat lugubrious *fin de siècle* taste in interior design is commemorated in a sequence of rooms nowadays shared by temporary exhibitions. You should try, if possible, to see the palace's topmost storey, the *soffitto*, in which the floors and ceiling timbers have been restored to their original appearance, and the view across roofs, terraces and canals is truly ravishing. Fortuny's real claim to celebrity was as the creator, with his wife Henriette, of the gauzy silk evening dresses and teagowns which graced the heroines of Proust and Colette in the early years of the present century. Their fabric was so delicately sinuous that it was said that you could easily pull one through a wedding ring.

Back in the Calle della Mandorla, cross the bridge (Ponte della Cortesia) with a glimpse to your right of fine mediaeval triple-windowed façades on the canal, and enter the Campo Manin. This used to be Campo San Paternian, but the church which formerly stood here only exists as a memory picked out in a plan marked on the pavement, and the square has been renamed to commemorate Daniele Manin, the Jewish lawyer who led the resistance to the Hapsburg government in 1848. An ardent lover of his native city, he had such an intimate knowledge of its streets and canals that once, when he was arrested by the Austrian police, blindfolded and flung into a gondola to be taken to a secret place for interrogation, he worked out exactly where he was by the various turnings of the boat. Brave and highminded, he stiffened Venice's nerve during the terrible siege of 1849, but, beaten at last by General Radetzky's army, spent his last few years in impoverished exile.

Opposite his statue, a lane leads down to Palazzo Contarini dal Bovolo, the work of Giovanni Candi (*c.* 1499), an exceedingly tall late-fifteenth-century building from which projects a massive spiral staircase behind curving arches and balustrades, known as a *scala a chiocciola* (snailshell stair) from its twisting shape. For sheer flamboyance of gesture there is certainly nothing like it in this part of the city, and its impact never fails as the unsuspecting visitor peers into the courtyard for the first time.

Return to the *campo* and walk past the modern Cassa di Risparmio bank building, which occupies the site of Aldus Manutius's fifteenth-century print works, where travellers inspecting the newest classical editions were often invited to lend a hand at the presses and crank out a page or two for themselves. Crossing Campo San Luca, whose bars are a favourite Venetian meeting place, turn left and then right, past the recently restored Teatro Goldoni. Over the bridge, in the thick of Venice's busiest shopping area and close by Campo San Bartolomeo, a popular open-air rendezvous for crowds of young people, you confront one of the city's oldest churches, though you would hardly guess this from the no-nonsense seventeenth-century façade, the work of the protean, omnicompetent Giuseppe Sardi.

San Salvador was founded a thousand years earlier, but the overall structure of the present church is a major example of Renaissance design, by Giorgio Spavento (d. 1509) who devised a conglomerate pattern of three Greek crosses, and Tullio Lombardo (d. 1532) whose achievement was rounded off in 1534 by Sansovino. Though Scamozzi, forty years afterwards, added little lanterns to the domes to let in light, the interior still remains quite dark, but the overall beauty of the relationship between the various curves and verticals makes this among the most impressive Venetian church interiors.

The aisles and transepts are rich in fine monuments, including Sansovino's tomb for the Doge Francesco Venier (1554–56), a triumphal arch flanked by figures of Faith and Charity, and the architecturally wayward memorial to Caterina Cornaro by Bernardino Contino (d. 1597). Caterina was one of the most fortunate women who ever lived. Born in 1454 to a 'first family' of Venice, she was married at the age of fourteen to James of Lusignan, whose forebears had been kings of Cyprus for over two centuries. When James died in 1473, Caterina found life as the widowed queen of an island full of contentious nobles increasingly difficult, and in 1489 she was prevailed upon to give up her domains to the Republic in return for being able to keep her royal statues and becoming chatelaine of a delightful palace at Asolo, in the hills north of Venice. There she held court among a group of admiring poets, painters and musicians, who coined the verb *asolare*, 'to enjoy the kind of sophisticated life led at Asolo', which later gave a title to that resident *asolano* Robert Browning for his last volume of verse, *Asolando*.

The other visual pleasure of San Salvador is provided by an exceptional late work from the hand of Titian (1488–1576), whose loyalty to Venice never wavered despite his international celebrity during the course of a long career. This is the large *Annunciation* over the third altar in the right aisle, where the artist's improvisatory, free-flowing final manner is shown at its best in his painting of the feathers on the wings of the tall, imposing angel who dominates the canvas.

Since shops and shopping form – or used to form – one of Venice's incidental delights, you may follow a time-honoured precedent by strolling through the Merceria (or Marzaria, as it is written in Venetian) to the left of the church, turning right at the bottom, and left into what eventually becomes the Merceria di San Zulian. In 1645 John Evelyn, walking these same streets, was frankly dazed by their assault on the various senses, writing rapturously of 'the most delicious streete in the World for the sweetnesse of it, being all the way on both sides, continually tapissry'd as it were, with Cloth of Gold, rich Damasks & other silks . . . to this add the perfumers & Apothecaries shops, and the innumerable cages of Nightingals, which they keepe, that entertaine you with their melody from shop to shop'. Nowadays there are no nightingales, far too many sellers of leather and glassware and a quite inexplicable number of shops displaying cheaply painted carnival masks, but the overall atmosphere can surely not have altered that much.

San Zulian, or San Giuliano, at the end of its eponymous Marzaria, is the only church in Venice whose outside you can walk right round. It was rebuilt by Tommaso Rangone, a doctor from Ravenna who claimed to be able to prolong life to the age of 120. In 1553 he commissioned Sansovino to create a façade culminating in a statue of him seated amid his books and globes, a monument to self-projection but a notable portrait in stone nevertheless. Rangone's last act was a deliberately theatrical funeral for himself (he was only eighty when he died) with the mourners wearing special robes and his own learned works open at specified pages on top of the coffin. Inside the dark church you will need to drop a coin into the lighting box to gain an adequate impression of the ceiling panels, centred on an *Apotheosis of Saint Julian* painted by Palma Giovane (Giacomo Nigretti, 1544–1628), one of those not-quite-first-rank painters who spoil their work by trying too hard. These panels, however, are effective within their setting, a handsome grid of gilded wooden spars refashioned during the eighteenth century.

Past this church, one summer day in 1310, wound the rebellious followers of Bajamonte Tiepolo, who had raised a popular revolt against the Doge and the Grand Council, aimed at securing more power for the common people. As the rebels turned into the street leading down to Saint Mark's Square, an old woman busy pounding spices in a pestle and mortar leaned out of her window to watch them pass. The mortar, falling on the head of the standard-bearer, knocked him dead, and the revolt suddenly turned into an undignified rout as Bajamonte and his men, suspecting treachery, turned and fled. As a reward the old woman and her descendants were allowed to live in the house for ever at a peppercorn rent, and after the last of them died in the nineteenth century, a relief of the dame, whose name was Giustina Rossi, was placed above the shop occupying the site, where you can still see it.

Behind San Giuliano lies the Campo della Guerra, among several places where friendly fights used to take place between members of neighbouring parishes. Cross the bridge, and take the first turn on your left, up the busy shopping street of the Salizzada San Lio, but instead of carrying on towards the Rialto, turn left and follow the dark, narrow lane until it brings you out in front of the church of Santa Maria della Fava. *Fava* means 'bean', but the beans in this case were actually cakes sold by a local pastrycook on All Souls' Day. The church itself is a straightforward early-eighteenth-century building, but though it is not often open, you should try to catch a glimpse of a sensitively handled *Virgin and Child with Saint Anne*, an early work, dated 1732, by the great Giambattista Tiepolo, and a highly idiosyncratic *St Philip Neri Praying to the Virgin* by Giovanni Battista Piazzetta (1682–1754). In histories of Venetian art this painter is always made to seem something of an odd man out, if only because of his doggedly distinctive style, created from a carefully limited palette of strong browns, deep blacks and dark yellows, and by a use of livid, creamy flesh colours. Recent exhibitions have underlined his essential difference from the prevailing decorative bravura of his rococo contemporaries, while revealing him as one of the most assured of eighteenth-century draughtsmen.

Go back down the lane, cross into Campo San Lio, over the canal and through the gloomy courtyard beyond (this used to feature two eloquently laconic graffiti, which in translation read 'I love Paolo', 'Well I don't'). Turning left brings you onto a bridge with an attractive prospect of crossing canals, beside the back of the Teatro Malibran. This is the oldest surviving theatre in Venice, though its interior, a restrained essay in the so-called 'Liberty' style (the Italian *art nouveau*, named after the famous Regent Street emporium), dates only from the turn of the present century. As the Teatro San Giovanni Grisostomo, under the patronage of the Grimani family, it witnessed the triumph, in 1710, of the opera *Agrippina*, composed by the 25-year-old George Frideric Handel (1685–1759) at the culminating point of a highly successful three years in Italy. The opera ran for an unprecedented twenty-seven performances, and on the first night the ecstatic Venetian audience hailed the young German genius, calling out, 'Long live the Saxon and blessed be the mother who bore him!'

Later the theatre fell on hard times, and during the early nineteenth century was threatened with closure. The manager had the inspired idea of inviting the star soprano Maria Malibran (1808–1836), appearing on another Venetian stage, to give a benefit concert. Malibran, the Maria Callas of her day and a legendary figure in the annals of romantic opera, readily agreed and waived any suggestion of a fee for her appearance. The concert was naturally a sell-out, and the theatre, its fortunes secured overnight, gratefully adopted the diva's name as its own.

Under a sequence of *sottoporteghi* to the left of the theatre are two rather grim, dingy courtyards, one of which features a battered *vera da pozzo* (well-head) and some intricately-carved Byzantine arches dating from the early twelfth century. These are the so-called *Corti del Milion*, where that hardiest of Venetian explorers Marco Polo was born in 1259 and is said to have lived on his return from China. When his book, dictated to a Pisan fellow prisoner with whom he had been captured by the Genoese and originally written in French, reached Venice, Marco's fellow citizens scoffed at the marvels of the East and his adventures at the court of Khan Kublai as a pack of lies, and called it *El Milion* for its million taradiddles. The name stuck to Marco as well, but it seems sad that his spectacular story (which after all is mostly founded on truth) should be commemorated by one of the most dismal spots in Venice.

Up the street is the church of San Giovanni Grisostomo, another of those Greek dedications (to the celebrated Byzantine preacher John Chrysostom – 'golden mouth') which constantly recall Venice's strong links with the Eastern empire. Built on the site of an earlier church between 1497 and 1501 to designs by Mauro Coducci, this is one of the purest examples of Renaissance architecture in Venice, ideally proportioned as a Greek cross embracing a dome at its axis. The revolting plastic altar candles should not put you off a close look at two exceptional pictures, by Giovanni Bellini and Sebastiano del Piombo. The former painted his *Saint Jerome, Saint Christopher and Saint Augustine* in 1513, towards the end of a career during which his lyrical genius had fixed a benchmark for Venetian painting and nurtured the talents of such major artists as Titian and Giorgione. Bellini was not vain enough to resent the influence of his pupils, and this altarpiece makes obvious allusions, in its shimmering verdure of landscape, to Giorgione's manner, perhaps as a conscious homage to the brilliant young master who had died three years earlier.

Sebastinao del Piombo (1485–1547) was one of comparatively few Venetian Renaissance artists who left his native city in search of work elsewhere in Italy. At the Papal court in Rome, he came strongly under the influence of Raphael and Michelangelo, but the early altarpiece here at San Giovanni Grisostomo reflects a Venetian softness and suppleness in its handling of the saints gathered around Saint John Chrysostom. Some of these figures may actually have been sketched by Giorgione himself, though the female group on the left is pure Sebastiano in its serene sense of a hidden knowledge carried within these calm countenances. Of the one turning outwards Henry James memorably wrote, 'Never was there a greater air of breeding, a deeper expression of tranquil superiority. She walks a goddess – as if she trod without sinking the waves of the Adriatic. It is impossible to conceive a more perfect expression of the aristocratic spirit either in its pride or in its benignity . . . But for all this there are depths of possible disorder in her light-coloured eye.'

The streets around the church are some of the busiest in Venice, and you will probably want to quit them as soon as possible, so turn to your right as you leave by the main entrance, and follow the street round to the left. Passing under the *sottoportego* and over the bridge will bring you out to a parting of the ways between more of the same shops and bars and something a good deal quieter and set apart from well-beaten tourist routes.

In front of you stands the little church of Santissimi Apostoli, or as it is generally abbreviated in Italian, SS. Apostoli, whose campanile's distinctive onion dome makes it more like something from eastern Europe than a specifically Venetian belltower. This is one of the oldest churches in the city, but the fabric of the present building is mainly sixteenth century and uninteresting, save for one remarkable feature. Off the right aisle is the Cappella Corner, the family chapel of Queen Caterina Cornaro, who was originally buried here before being moved to San Salvador. Built in the form of a domed *tempietto* or small temple, to a design by Tullio Lombardo, it dates from around 1540 and encloses monuments to Caterina's father and uncle. On the altar is a small painting of *The Last Communion of Saint Lucy*, painted around 1747 by Giambattista Tiepolo. The drama of the episode, foreshadowing the young girl's martyrdom which began by her being blinded, is evoked through a deliberately huddled grouping of the foreground figures and by the inquisitive pose of an onlooker peering from the balcony. Tiepolo's personal style, so markedly different in oils from the airy 'soft-focus' manner of his fresco painting, is superbly exemplified here in the play of light across the various costumes – for the scene is essentially a piece of theatre – and in the vigorous brushwork.

From Campo SS. Apostoli, turn right, along the Salizzada del Pistor and the Calle dei Proverbi. Cross the bridge, from the Fondamenta dei Sartori where you can see a bas-relief of a kind typical throughout Venice, showing the Blessed Virgin spreading her cloak in protection of a group of kneeling worshippers. In this case it is the Tailors' Guild, whose Ospedale dei Sartori once stood here, and whose patrons, Saints Barbara and Omobono, are also featured in the relief. Beyond the bridge you pass the grave Gothic Palazzo Sceriman, named after a patrician family who originally came to Venice as Armenian merchants. Over another canal you arrive at last in the long Campo dei Gesuiti, and prepare to enter one of the most bizarre spaces ever devised for the worship of God and His saints.

The Jesuit Order was never popular in Venice, if only because of the city's historically problematic relationship with the Pope, to whom the Society of Jesus was directly responsible. By its very nature, republican Venice jibbed at any authority which pretended to power over an ancient independent state on a basis of spiritual blackmail. An inevitable consequence, as Rome felt its supremacy weakening and went on the defensive during the late-sixteenth-century Counter-Reformation, was a head-on collision between La Serenissima and Holy Church, culminating in the wholesale condemnation, in 1606, of the Venetian state to a papal interdict.

Thus the Jesuits were only grudgingly permitted a toehold in metropolitan Venice, ironically one of the most fervently Catholic cities in Italy, but one which resented any suggestion that its freedoms and privileges should be subjected to the ultimate jurisdiction of Rome. The church of the Gesuiti has always maintained a curious sense of isolation, the feeling of a community if not in exile, then banished physically to the fringes of a grand and prosperous metropolis, as if to keep its distance and know its place in the singular Venetian order of things.

It was only in 1657 that the Jesuits acquired the site for the present church, which included former monastic buildings (later turned into a military barracks and now converted into flats), and commissioned Giovanni Battista Fattoretto (dates unknown) to create a stately Baroque façade, peopled with statues of the Twelve Apostles, which from a distance always have an oddly menacing air, like sentries on lookout duty.

For the interior, the dissolute Swiss architect Domenico Rossi (1678–1742) presumably took his cue from the epoch-making church of the Gesù in Rome, where the emphasis of both structure and decoration had been consciously placed on surface ornament to induce a kind of religious intoxication, leaving the worshipper with no choice but to fall prostrate in bedazzled amazement. At first glance it looks as though the walls are made

entirely from the heavy damask, velvet and brocade whose weaving was such a noted speciality among the Venetians. There are folds, there are fringes, there are tassels, there are patterns of flowers and leaves, and a veritable sense of a nap in the texture, as if rubbing a hand across it might reveal a sheen of gold beneath – yet everything here is created from green and white marble, furnished at vast expense by a nouveau riche patrician family eager to display both its devotion and its bank balance.

Doubtless these extraordinary marble upholsteries made a dramatic impact on the original crowd of the faithful who entered the church on its completion in 1729, though nowadays, in the context of a lonely corner of a half-dead city on the edge of a quiet lagoon, the Gesuiti appears irredeemably sad in its gelid, damp emptiness. Even the colourful ceiling panels by Francesco Fontebasso (1709–1769) in their white and gold stucco frames cannot quite take the chill off the atmosphere. According to William Dean Howells in his *Venetian Life* (1866) the only thing which does that is the sinister fire under the gridiron at the centre of Titian's *Martyrdom of Saint Lawrence*, which you will find in the first chapel on the left. A late work, painted around 1558 to honour a dead friend named for the saint, this is the direct ancestor of all those 'night pieces' which so entranced the imagination of artists during the following century. Its *dramatis personae* do not in themselves matter half as much as the various flecks and smudges of light falling into the well of deep shadow engulfing the scene.

Titian lived close by, at a time when this part of Venice was still full of orchards and gardens sloping down to the shore. For one of the quietest of Venetian walks, you can stroll out onto the Fondamenta Nuove and look across to the islands of San Michele and Murano, seen best on a summer morning when you are still cool from immersion in the marble fantasmagoria of the Gesuiti and a breeze stirs the blue expanse of water. Otherwise, turning left and then right will bring you to a fine cluster of Renaissance palaces unique, so far as I know, among patrician *palazzi* for having been designed by their owner (Franceso Zen, who died in 1538). Past the old church of Santa Caterina, permanently closed for a restoration which will probably never take place, turn left along Calle Racchetta, go under the *sottoportego* and over the bridge.

Turning right will eventually bring you out opposite the Scuola Nuova della Misericordia, a large unfinished project by Sansovino, begun in 1532. This stands at the head of one of three parallel canals which quarter the northwestern *sestiere* of the city, the district known as Cannaregio, 'where the bamboo canes grow', one of the areas least visited by tourists. Historically this was never one of the more fashionable zones of Venice, and though it has its share of noble dwellings and two or three splendid churches, the essence of Cannaregio is what Italians call '*un quartiere popolare*', a corner of the town where the real life of ordinary working Venetians still manages to hang on.

In the nineteenth century these alleys and courts (there are very few small side canals in this part of Venice) were even quieter, more melancholy and run down. Théophile Gautier in 1850 wrote of 'crumbling houses whose windows are filled by wooden planks, deserted squares, empty spaces with clothes hanging out to dry and a few ragged children at play, desolate boatyards where vessels are being caulked amid clouds of thick smoke, abandoned churches battered by Austrian shells', while the Goncourt brothers, Edmond and Jules, arriving a few years later, compared the scruffy, frowzy, tatterdemalion air of Cannaregio to that of 'some antique sculpture eroded by the sun and rain'. Not for nothing, therefore, will you feel like an explorer here, unlikely as you are to encounter many other adventurous fellow spirits. The pleasure, up at this end of the city, is almost exclusively reserved for those observant, inquisitive souls who are curious as to how Venice looks in its less ceremonial, more reach-me-down guise.

Follow the Fondamenta della Misericordia all the way along to the Calle Larga and cross the bridge to Campo dei Mori, which is named after a *fondaco* or warehouse of Arab merchants which used to stand here. The three rather battered statues, set into the wall opposite the bridge and resting on fragments of Roman masonry, are said to represent three Greek traders from the Peloponnese, named Rioba, Sandi and Alfani, who arrived in Venice in 1112, adopted the surname of Mastelli and built the large Gothic palace at the end of the *campo*, fronting the canal (the precious camel with which they made their fortunes in the Levant is commemorated in relief on the façade). Rioba's effigy, nearest to the bridge, became a sort of folk totem for the people of Cannaregio, and whenever a lampoon or a scurrilous rhyme ran around the city, its authorship was always ascribed to 'Sior Antonio Rioba'.

On the *fondamenta* to the right of the bridge a plaque marks the house where Tintoretto spent the last twenty years of a busy and prolific career. Only recently have adequate cleaning and restoration applied to his major works in Venice brought back to us the surreal, dream-architectural quality of his imagination, whose profoundly spiritual basis is easily forgotten if we think of him merely as a jobbing painter amid the sensual worldliness of sixteenth-century Venetian life. Ruskin, as so often, looked beyond this context into the very essence of Tintoretto's inspirations, and dragged his wife Effie up here to this quiet backwater of Cannaregio one hot day to the painter's parish church of the Madonna dell'Orto to look at 'two large Tintorets', an experience she emphatically did not relish.

Few of us are likely to turn and run, as Effie did, from the Madonna dell'Orto, newly restored by the British Venice in Peril Fund as one of mediaeval Venice's most arresting churches. Begun around 1350 by Fra Tiberio of Parma, and named after a miraculous image of the Virgin discovered in a nearby garden (*orto*), the building received its richly detailed façade a century later, with the Delle Masegne brothers contributing the fine sequence of apostles in rows of little niches above the tall, slender-shafted four-light windows and Bartolomeo Bon adding the porch in 1483.

Inside, the layout is extremely simple, a nave with side altars (one of which boasts a reliquary containing a kneecap of Saint

Christopher) but without aisles, and an apse with chapels behind Greek marble columns. Apart from the exquisite small early Bellini Madonna in the first chapel on the left, and a somewhat overrestored *Saint John the Baptists with Saints* by Cima da Conegliano (1459–1518), what we, like the Ruskins, come to see are the Tintorettos, more especially the two massive works on either side of the highaltar, painted in 1546, when, at twenty-eight, the artist was beginning to stretch his genius to its fullest. On the left is *The Worship of the Golden Calf*, often taken as an allegory of thoughtless Venetian hedonism turning its back on spiritual truths embodied by the Ten Commandments, carried down by angels to a cloudborne Moses. On the right is one of the most thunderously dramatic, not to say melodramatic Last Judgments ever painted, in which Tintoretto fuses the Christian apocalypse with elements from classical Greek mythology, including Charon's Stygian ferry. This was clearly too frightening for poor Effie Ruskin, but her husband's pen rises magnificently to the challenge. 'Batlike, out of the holes and caverns and shadows of the earth the bones gather, and the clay heaps heave, rattling and adhering into half-kneaded anatomies, that crawl and startle and struggle up among the putrid weeds, with the clay clinging to their clotted hair, and their heavy eyes sealed by the earth-darkness.'

There are other paintings by Tintoretto in the church, including a cunningly-lit *Presentation of the Virgin* above the door of the sacristy, formerly attributed to his son Domenico. Both of them are buried in the chapel to the right of the apse, along with Domenico's sister Marietta, whose death at an early age devastated not merely her family, but the whole city. Her father's pupil, she was regarded as a prodigy of talent both in painting and in music, but instead of accepting invitations to the courts of King Philip II of Spain and the Hapsburg Emperor Maximilian, she married a Venetian jeweller, who encouraged her to paint portraits of her family and friends rather than flattering likenesses of the rich and famous. It seems likely that Tintoretto came to

63

view his work at the Madonna dell'Orto as a kind of memorial to the young Marietta, so untimely lost.

Outside the church to your left at the end of the *fondamenta* is Palazzo Contarini dal Zaffo, a noble late Renaissance building which provided the setting for gatherings of writers, scholars and connoisseurs under the aegis of the cultivated Contarini family. Kindred spirits also met to discuss art and literature in the small pink-and-white Casino degli Spiriti, which stands just behind the palace, on the point looking towards the island of San Michele. Owing to a muddle over the implications of the name, an entirely baseless legend has been devised in connection with spirits of another sort, supposedly haunting this house. Once, goes the old tale, a Venetian gentleman lived there, whose wife had an affair with his best friend, godfather to his eldest child. When her lover died, she pined away also, and at midnight on the day of her death, as the maid sat watching by the corpse, the shade of the loved one entered the room, touched the dead woman lightly on the arm and signed to her to get up. Horrified, the servant watched as the revived cadaver arose and dressed itself. Then the ghastly pair, beckoning the maid to precede them with a lantern, slipped downstairs and out of the house, dashing the light from the girl's hand and leaving her in a swoon.

In the opposite direction from Palazzo Contarini, you cross the canal and walk up Calle Loredan onto the Fondamenta della Sensa. From here, a detour might be made down Calle del Capitello to look at the church of Sant'Alvise, dating from 1388 and built as an act of piety by Antonia, daughter of Doge Antonio Venier, in response to a vision of Saint Louis of Toulouse. Alvise (Aloysius) is the Venetian form of Louis and used to be a cherished patrician name, though nowadays it has been appropriated by humbler folk for baptizing their sons. I say 'a detour might be made', since this church, in its grass-grown *campo*, is never open, even if reproductions suggest that its two paintings by Giambattista Tiepolo, painted in 1738, are worth a glimpse. Both are on Passion themes, a *Christ Crowned with Thorns* and an astonishing *Flagellation*, in which the scoffers and mockers in the background are shown wearing the traditional Venetian *bauta*, the carnival mask with its beetling eyebrows and hooked nose.

If Sant'Alvise turns out to be shut, retrace your steps, go over the canal and up Calle della Malvasia (which takes its name from the malmsey wine produced at Monemvasia in southern Greece), turn left along Fondamenta degli Ormesini (sellers of cloth from Ormuz in the Persian Gulf) and cross the bridge which brings you at last into Campo del Ghetto Nuovo. This is the parent of all other ghettoes in the world, since the name derives from the Italian verb *gettare*, meaning 'to smelt iron', an activity originally carried on here before the area was turned over to the Jews in 1516. There had been Jewish families settled in Venice since the early Middle Ages, mostly on the island of Giudecca, but their commercial success excited considerable envy among Christian merchants (the roots of Shakespeare's story of Shylock, Antonio and the pound of flesh lie here) and a whole series of laws was passed to restrict their activities and limit them to a special quarter, one which had the advantage, as far as the government was concerned, of being shut off by canals on three of its four sides.

Jews lived somewhat more securely in Venice and its mainland towns than elsewhere throughout Italy, though genuine anti-Semitism among Italians has, until recently, been rare, and the nation's record in protecting fugitives from Nazi persecution during World War Two was a fairly honourable one. The Venetian Republic, while not exactly cherishing the Jews, appreciated their importance as traders, moneylenders and doctors, but expected them to wear a distinguishing costume and forbade any who converted to Christianity to set foot any longer within a practising Jewish household.

The first ghetto area was inevitably much too small to accommodate the flood of refugees from Germany, with its long traditions of persecution, and Portugal, where the Inquisition, during the sixteenth century, developed a morbid obsession with hunting out clandestine Judaism. Even when the community spread along the neighbouring street (somewhat confusingly known as Ghetto Vecchio, 'the old ghetto') and surrounding lanes, its members were forced to build upwards rather than outwards, and some of these tall skyscraper houses still remain around the Campo del Ghetto Nuovo. Here the Jews survived, amid considerable squalor, in a spot where, as one French traveller noted, 'all the forgotten maladies of some Oriental lazarhouse seemed to gnaw at the blistered walks', until Napoleon's enlightened decree liberated them, with full civil rights at last.

No less than five magnificent synagogues survive, each representing one of the national points of origin from which the community originally came together. The Scuola Spagnola, in Ghetto Vecchio, built in 1555, was probably given its present sumptuously Baroque interior by Baldassare Longhena a century later, though a further restoration was needed in 1849, when it was hit by a shell during the Austrian bombardment. Directly opposite is the Scuola Levantina, completed in 1561, richly adorned with gilding, deep red damask and silver lamps, with the *bimah* or rostrum under a lofty *baldacchino*, the creation of Andrea Brustolon (1662–1732), the greatest woodcarver of his generation, who came from the upland town of Belluno north of Venice, where much of his best work can still be seen. In Ghetto Nuovo stands the rather severe synagogue of those Jews who came originally from the Italian mainland, and nearby, currently being restored, is the Scuola Canton, begun in 1531 and named after the French community, who referred to their houses as *canton des juifs*. Next to this is the most august temple of them all, the lovely oval Scuola Tedesca, for the northern Ashkenazy, founded in 1528, with white balustrades and mottled marble panels. Attached to it is a small Jewish museum.

Miraculously the community survived the Nazi occupation, though 250 Jews were deported to concentration camps, including the chief rabbi and twenty bedridden inmates of an old-people's home. Nowadays the whole area is a tranquil shadow of its former over-peopled liveliness, in the age when Thomas Coryate (who had of course never set eyes on a Jew in his native Elizabethan England) came to stare at the worshippers in the synagogue, noting some of them to be 'most sweet-featured persons, which gave me occasion the more to lament their religion', especially the women, 'whereof some were as beautiful as ever I saw, and so gorgeous in their apparel, jewels, chaines of gold, and rings adorned with precious stones, that some of our English Countesses do scarce exceed them'. Typically, crazy Tom, of Oddcombe in Devon, who later walked all the way to Delhi and back, got into a religious argument with 'the Jewish Rabbin', and had to be rescued by a secretary of the British ambassador Sir Henry Wotton, who just happened to be passing in his gondola.

Wotton, an exceptionally gifted man, whose love of poetry and music endeared him to John Donne, lived on the Fondamenta degli Ormesini, in a palace where much of the furniture was hired from the Jews. They made such a profit from the transaction that it was said that they 'looked for his return as they hoped for the coming of Messiah'. As King James I's envoy to the Most Serene Republic, he was not always happy in his work, if only because the state, whatever the honour done to foreign embassies, viewed them with deep suspicion, and forbade patricians to have anything to do with them. We can scarcely blame Wotton for growing a trifle cynical as regards his profession, which he defined as being that of 'a man sent to lie abroad for the good of his country', a *double entendre* on the two meanings of the word 'lie' which angered his royal master so much that Wotton had to write two fulsome public apologies in Latin before he was forgiven.

Cannaregio was always a popular place with ambassadors, probably because, until the end of the eighteenth century at least, its various gardens gave it a rural flavour, and its exposed position on the curve of the city's northernmost island meant that the streets and canals had the benefit of the fresh breezes off the lagoon. Once you recall that its larger waterways all run in dead straight lines, you can hardly lose your way, should you fancy a ramble through its humbler *calli* north of the Ghetto. These will give you some idea of workaday Venice, without shops, hotels, restaurants or tourists, an area whose atmosphere has not greatly changed since Gaetano Zompini (1702–1778) published his engravings of such characteristic street types as '*el codega*', the man who carried a lantern down dark alleys ahead of benighted travellers, and Jan Grevembrock (1731–1807) painted his cheerful watercolours of boatmen and market folk.

If, on the other hand, you yearn for noise and crowds, leave the Ghetto by its western approach from the Fondamenta di Cannaregio and walk up to the Ponte delle Guglie, a bridge tricked out with an elegant set of obelisks, built in 1580. Crossing this will bring you out into Campo San Geremia, in front of the church of the same name. This is an august eighteenth-century adaptation of Santa Maria della Salute (see page 163) by Carlo Corbellini (dates unknown), an architect from Brescia, a town on the very edge of the Republic's territories which has its fair share of such handsome churches. San Geremia was seriously damaged by Austrian bombardment during the 1848–9 siege, but retains several attractive marble altars and shelters the body of Saint Lucy behind the high altar. Like many of Venice's other saints, the holy corpse was looted, in this case from Syracuse in Sicily where her martydom originally took place. Until the Hapsburg government brought the railway across the lagoon, she lay in a church designed by Palladio on the site of the present station, which is named after her. A slightly shamefaced inscription on the outer wall of San Geremia fronting the Grand Canal tells us that Venice and the world implore the saint to grant them peace. Even in this spot, however, the hapless patron of sufferers from eye disease, whose feast falls on the darkest day of the year, 21st December, has not been allowed to rest in quiet. Some time ago the body was stolen, and has only recently been recovered.

At right angles to the church stands the tremendous Istrian marble façade of Palazzo Labia, the work of Andrea Cominelli (1720) though the building itself is by Alessandro Tremignon, completed around 1750. A sequence of grand courtyards and staircases, it was created for a nouveau riche banker, who was in the habit of demonstrating his wealth to dinner guests by throwing the silver dishes off which they had eaten into the canal,

accompanied by the punning exclamation '*L'abbia o non l'abbia, saro sempre Labia!*' – 'Whether I have it or not, I'll always be Labia!' Needless to add, a net had been stretched beneath the water, in which the silver was collected for use in further displays of conspicuous consumption.

Labia commissioned Giambattista Tiepolo and his assistant Girolamo Mengozzi Colonna to put the finishing touches to the palace in a set of frescoes which constitute, for many who see them, the ultimate expression of eighteenth-century decor at its most confident and unselfconscious. Within a brilliantly contrived architectural *trompe l'oeil* of illusory perspectives, we see Cleopatra banqueting with Mark Antony on their first meeting at Ephesus, amid gorgeously dressed servants and courtiers, and her embarkation for Egypt, with the god Aeolus and his attendant winds hovering to provide favourable breezes. The whole wondrous confection is the more remarkable for its assertiveness in an age when Venice was supposed to be tottering to its knees politically and materially, and for its deliberate appeal to the manner of Paolo Veronese, who had died a century and a half earlier, but whose costumes and poses are directly imitated here, perhaps partly in a nostalgic reminiscence of braver days, when more people than *arriviste* plutocrats could have commissioned such grandiose schemes from Tiepolo.

Nowadays Palazzo Labia is the home of the local branch of RAI, the Italian state broadcasting service, but during the late 1940s and 1950s it belonged to a fabulously rich Argentinian, Carlos Beistegui, known to the international *beau monde* as Charlie, who had the inspired idea of holding, in September 1951, a grand costume ball which should mirror the hedonistic delights Tiepolo had painted on the walls. This was, by all accounts, the last great party in Venice, a masquerade involving the distinguished clientele of Harry's Bar, a gaggle of millionaires, a generous sprinkling of aristocrats, several of the smartest of that season's visitors, and a horde of *paparazzi* with their cameras, 'and, of course, every dressmaker and pansy in the world', as the American diplomat's wife Susan Mary Allsop succinctly put it.

70

The undoubted star of the occasion was Lady Diana Cooper, fresh from her triumphs at the Paris embassy and now appearing as Tiepolo's Cleopatra, in a gondola, attended by black pages. Mrs Allsop watched enraptured as 'she turned on the landing wharf to look down at the scene, and I don't think I ever saw anything more beautiful than that – the light from the palace windows falling on her face and the pearls and the blonde hair . . . her dress was blue brocade, very *décolletée* and in shape just like the picture'. Poor Charlie Beistegui did not live long to enjoy his triumph, growing melancholy and committing suicide soon afterwards.

From the palace, go back over the bridge and along Rio Terra San Leonardo (a *rio terra* is an earthed-in canal), turn right down Calle Colonna, then left along Calle del Cristo, which will bring you out behind (or *drio*, as the Venetians say) the church of San Marcuola. This is one of those Venetian contractions – San Trovaso and San Stae are others – which uses one name to hide an entirely different one. Or in this case two, since what looks like a dedication to little Saint Mark is actually the church of the martyrs Hermagoras and Fortunatus, bundled up, Lord knows how, into this single denomination. The pair figure in statues on the high altar by Giammaria Morlaiter (1699–1782), one of several eminent hands who contributed to the decoration of this austere classical building by Giorgio Massari (dates unknown) completed in 1736, all except for its façade, which was never added to the bare brick front onto the Grand Canal. On the left-hand wall of the chancel is a powerfully drawn *Last Supper*, painted in 1547 by the young Tintoretto.

At the eastern end of the church a simple leger stone commemorates a composer who during his lifetime was among the most famous musicians in the world, more celebrated even than his great contemporaries Bach, Handel and Mozart, but whose star sank into total oblivion when he was barely cold in his tomb here at San Marcuola. Johann Adolf Hasse (1699–1783), born near Hamburg and always known in his adoptive Italy as 'the Saxon' (like Handel at San Giovanni Grisostomo indeed), was seen by many as the most important opera composer of his day, and his long career, stretching from a spell as musician in the royal chapel at Naples, via the palaces of Dresden, to the imperial court of Vienna, was one of uninterrupted triumph. He married the star soprano Faustina Bordoni, who had enchanted the audiences of London's Haymarket in several Handelian roles specially composed for her, and the pair returned to her home town of Venice to spend their last years in dignified retirement. Recently Hasse's music has been dusted off, emerging as lively, tuneful, perfectly tailor-made for singers, but ultimately rather heartless and shallow.

Across the little canal from San Marcuola, in the direction of the Rialto, stands the palace where Hasse's lineal heir in the operative field, a far greater artist but an infinitely less likeable man, died on 11th February, 1883. Richard Wagner, with all his loathing of Italian music (except that of Bellini, which he saw as foreshadowing his own), was the very last person who might have been expected to enjoy Venice, but he had come here in search of a mild winter climate and the comforts of the entresol of Palazzo Vendramin Calergi, whose sixteenth-century façade by Mauro Coducci punctuates this section of the Grand Canal so distinctively.

Whatever his seminal influence on modern music, Wagner was a repulsive creature, egomaniacal, manipulative and entirely without moral principles. His last days, surrounded by an entourage whom his mysterious basilisk attractiveness kept loyal even while they hated and feared him, were devoted to a litany of grumbles and complaints, the production of several long theoretical essays full of the kind of half-baked racial and genetic ideas which later played their part in the rise of Nazism, and the contemplation of an opera on Buddhist themes. For his wife Cosima's birthday he arranged a performance of his woeful early attempt at a symphony in the manner of Beethoven, a work upon which she ventured the supremely tactful judgment that 'it is the music of one who knows no fear'. He died in her arms, in a room which is still shown inside the palace, now a municipal casino.

Up the lane (Calle Vendramin) you enter Rio Terra della Maddalena, passing the interesting hexagonal church of La Maddalena on your right, built by the hydraulic engineer Tommaso Temanza (1705–1789) as a neo-classical domed tabernacle, but nowadays kept perpetually locked against worshippers and tourists alike. Turning the corner, you come out opposite the not especially arresting church of Santa Fosca, over whose *campo* broods the statue of Pietro Paolo Sarpi (1552–1625), a figure of whom Venice ought to be – and indeed probably is – seriously proud.

Sarpi was a monk of the Servite order, whose comprehensive intelligence and deep learning brought him to doubt the arrogant claims made by the Papacy during the interdict of 1606, when he was commissioned to put Venice's case to the world. So brilliantly was this defence conducted that Rome had no choice but to back down, and Protestants all over Europe hailed him as essentially one of their own. He became a hero to the English as 'Peter-Paul Sarpi' and Sir Henry Wotton went to call on him in his monastic cell, where he sat 'fenced with a castle of paper about his chair and over his head'. The learned friar seems to have been one of those rare and admirable Catholics who kept their faith while refusing to submit their intellectual lives to the tyranny of dogma and papal authority.

Naturally he was loathed by the Roman hierarchy, who conveniently ignored their Christian vocation in plotting to get rid of him by whatever means. Around five o'clock on the evening of the 5th October, 1607, Sarpi was walking towards the convent through the autumn twilight, accompanied by two friends. As he crossed the bridge at the end of Campo Santa Fosca, he was set upon by five *bravi*, hit-men who stabbed him again and again, only running away when a lethal dagger-thrust went through his right ear and lodged in the upper cheekbone. Miraculously Sarpi, tended by the Republic's best doctors, survived, later making the grim pun that he recognized the *style* (meaning also *stylus* or pointed weapon) of the Papal Curia in the murder attempt.

After Santa Fosca you enter the busy shopping street of Strada Nova, where there is almost nothing to halt your progress towards Santissimi Apostoli and the Rialto. Nothing, that is, unless you turn down the little lane on the right side, where a sign points towards the Ca'd'Oro. Ca' is a Venetian shortening of the Italian *casa* (house) and *oro* means gold, always a well-loved commodity in Venice and here used to adorn the palace built by Marino Contarini between 1421 and 1437. Deemed by many to be the perfect embodiment of that fusion between Gothic and Oriental motifs which typifies Venice at the height of her power as a trading nation, the building, with its graceful loggia opening onto the Grand Canal through four tall ogival arches, was the joint achievement of a group of Lombard masons working with Giovanni Bon and his son the great Bartolomeo.

The Ca'd'Oro survived more or less intact until the early nineteenth century, when the star dancer Marie Taglioni (1804–1884) was given it as a present by her lover Prince Troubetzkoi. Though scarcely a beauty (she was squat, with long arms and big shoulders) Taglioni had captivated Europe with her amazing technical versatility, and having fixed on retirement at the age of forty, she settled down in Venice to enjoy it to the full. The palace was effectively gutted, much of the marble decoration was stripped away, and, worst crime of all, the mediaeval outdoor staircase was removed altogether.

Only when the great Jewish financier Baron Franchetti acquired the building at the turn of the present century were efforts made to restore it to something like its original layout and appearance. Franchetti went to considerable lengths in tracking down original decorative features which La Taglioni, more interested in comfort than good taste, had been quick to get rid of. In the resuscitated Ca'd'Oro the Baron hung his exceptionally fine art collection, which subsequently passed to the state in 1927 under the terms of his will.

Here you will find one of the most absorbing displays in Venice of Renaissance sculpture. Look, for example, at the reliefs grouped in the long first-floor room known as the *portego*, more especially those by Andrea Briosco, known as Il Riccio (1470–1532), a thoroughgoing classical humanist from Padua,

74

and the powerfully characterized busts on the floor above by Alessandro Vittoria (1524–1608). A pupil of Sansovino, or at any rate working beside him, Vittoria became the doyen of sixteenth-century Venetian sculptors, and you will come across his unmistakable touch in statuary throughout the city, most notably at San Salvador and San Giorgio Maggiore.

Among Baron Franchetti's pictures are a most eloquent Saint Sebastian, a late work by Andrea Mantegna (1431–1506), whose pathos is effectively enhanced by its poised sculptural grace, and several fragments of fresco detached from the exterior walls of palaces and churches. There were many such decorations undertaken during the Renaissance, most notably on the façades of the Fondaco dei Tedeschi, the warehouse of the German merchants by the Rialto Bridge. The building is now the central post office, but a piece or two of Titian's Judith and Holofernes survives on the east wall. What remains of Giogione's frescoes for the Fondaco – a single female nude – is here in the gallery of the Ca'd'Oro.

You have left Cannaregio far behind, and the crowd in the Strada Nova now swirls you relentlessly back towards SS. Apostoli and the hum of the Rialto. Yet maybe something of the district's slightly forlorn charm has lodged in the memory, and you feel a sympathy with the singer of an old Venetian love song:

Butite sul balcon e dame un segno,
Ma no badar che sia da Cannaregio;
Ma no badar che la strada sia lunga,
Che un cuor che se vol ben presto se agionga.

'Come out onto the balcony and grant me a sign. Don't worry that I'm from Cannaregio and the way is long, for a loving heart will soon get there.'

4 : To Byzantium and Back

Sooner or later, visitors to Venice begin trying to match their visual experiences of the city with those of its artists, more particularly the famous *vedutisti*, 'view-painters', of the eighteenth century. A glance along the Grand Canal will suddenly conjure up a canvas by Canaletto (1697–1768), the most famous of them all, whose real name was Antonio Canal and whose early training, as the son of a theatrical scene painter, is reflected in the carefully composed, always somewhat detached images he produced for the delight of visiting English noblemen on the Grand Tour. So popular indeed was he with these *milords* that he made two visits to England, producing memorable views of London, Windsor and Warwick.

Altogether more subtle in his Venetian moods was Francesco Guardi (1712–1793), descended from one of the many families of painters living in the Alpine region along the Republic's northern frontier. Guardi's *vedute* take us out into the lagoon, showing misty glimpses of distant campanili and black gondolas among the scattered islands. Where Canaletto's world is always intensely peopled, bustling with gondoliers and their passengers and the daily toings and froings across bridges and squares, Guardi somehow manages to distil a sense of that haunting solitude which you can still find only a boatride away from the populous hum of city life around Saint Mark's.

It was in the Piazzetta itself that the *vedutisti* liked to paint what soon became a favourite Venetian view, a prospect towards the islands of San Giorgio and the Giudecca, framed by the two columns with the lion and Saint Theodore. The earliest of them, Canaletto's teacher Luca Carlevaris (1665–1731), made something of a speciality of this, but seems to have been equally entranced by the painterly possibilities of the great broad waterfront of the Riva degli Schiavoni, stretching northwards from the Doge's Palace in a gentle curve along the edge of the innermost lagoon, called the Bacino di San Marco.

In Carlevaris's day the Riva was a vast huddle of shipping, galleys, frigates, brigs, barques, various small Venetian oared boats like the *sandalo* and the *caorlina*, as well as, of course, dozens of gondolas. Perhaps the human crowd is not quite so varied now – there are no longer any Greeks in their *fustanella* cloaks and gold-embroidered jackets, Albanians in red bonnets, or long-robed, baggy-trousered Turks – and the boats moored along the quays are mostly cruiseliners, police launches or visiting battleships fresh from naval exercises. Yet the flavour is still essentially the same, the sense endures that Venice as a port is by no means dead, and the sea breeze which lifts the heat off the old stones as you walk makes a summer morning stroll here one of the most delectable of Venetian experiences.

The Riva degli Schiavoni took its name from the Slavic sailors from Dalmatia who made landfall on this shore at the end of their Adriatic voyages. Further Balkan associations are preserved in the names of the two narrow, rather fetid streets passed on your left, once you have crossed the Ponte della Paglia beside the Doge's Palace. Calle degli Albanesi speaks for itself: its neighbour, Calle delle Rasse, preserves a memory of Serbian merchants who sold a coarse woollen cloth called *rassa*, used to make gondola canopies.

The modern building on the left corner of this street replaces a group of humble one-storey houses which, in various forms, had occupied the site since the year 1172. They had been placed here by the Grand Council, partly in atonement and partly as a warning, after the murderers of Doge Vitale Michiel had tried to hide in the upper floors of a tall palace, promptly pulled down.

On the right-hand corner is the seriously magnificent Palazzo Dandolo, all fifteenth-century ogival windows and admirals' crockets on the parapet, a building much better known in its modern guise of the Albergo Danieli. The palace became a hotel in 1822, taking its name from the first manager, Signor Dal Niel, and from the start was viewed as the best of its kind in Venice. Charles Dickens, whom an initial encounter with the city sent into a crazy ecstasy, stayed here in 1846, the Ruskins arrived three years later, and Wagner and Proust were among other distinguished guests. The most notorious romance attached to the Danieli took place during the winter of 1833–34. In December the 24-year-old Alfred de Musset, already one of the *enfants terribles* of the late-flowering French Romantic movement, arrived with his mistress, the novelist George Sand, who had made a name for herself in the Parisian literary world as a rebel against contemporary notions of what a virtuous woman ought to be by deserting her worthless, drunken husband and donning male attire.

Venice in winter is rheumatic as much as romantic, and Musset promptly fell ill. The old doctor brought in to tend him was accompanied by a handsome young pupil, Pietro Pagello, whose charms were not lost on Madame Sand. Though, as a nineteenth-century French guidebook politely remarks, 'she never left the bedside while the invalid was in danger', Musset recovered from fever and delirium to find that Sand and Pagello had begun a passionate affair. In literary terms, however, the honours were decidedly hers, for while Musset produced a handful of pleasing little verses capturing the flavour of Venetian folksong, Sand's *Lettres d'un Voyageur* is an entirely candid reflection of her emotional crisis against backgrounds of travel.

Over the bridge beyond the Danieli is Albergo Paganelli, where Henry James, that most intensely empathetic of honorary Venetians, stayed in 1881, occupying a room on the fourth floor, where he finished *The Portrait of a Lady*. 'The waterside life,' he wrote, 'the wondrous lagoon spread before me, and the ceaseless human chatter of Venice came in at my windows, to which I seem to myself to have been constantly driven, in the fruitless fidget of composition.'

Turning left under the *sottoportego* by the hotel will take you down into Campo San Zaccaria, a square formed by rows of houses on the south and east sides, the old portico of the former Benedictine conventual cemetery to the west, the convent itself (later turned into a barracks) and, dominating everything, the looming early Renaissance façade of San Zaccaria, begun in 1444 by Antonio Gambello (d. 1481) and completed in much grander style between 1480 and 1500 by Mauro Coducci. The whole design, as determined by Coducci, is an ascending sequence of curved window arches, to culminate in a single deeply incised rose window above the topmost storey, balanced below by gently curved buttresses.

The convent itself was among the oldest, richest and, it was always rumoured, most corrupt monastic institutions in Venice, much favoured as a comfortable refuge by the daughters of the aristocracy. In return for having ceded part of its garden, on the edge of Piazza San Marco, the Doges honoured the place with an annual visit, in their coronation robes, to pay respects to the memory of eight of their earliest predecessors buried here. You can see the remains of the first church where they lay, preserved under the floor of the present apse and entered down a flight of steps in the chapel at the end of the right aisle.

Essentially San Zaccaria, attractive mixture of mediaeval and

Renaissance though it appears, retains its ancient layout, though the oldest thing here, apart from the remains of Zaccarias himself, is probably the body of Saint Athanasius, the bishop of Alexandria whose death in 373 ended a stormy career spent fighting heresy among the early Christians. He is displayed above the second altar on the right, in a floridly decorated silver casket, and is presumably yet another morsel of sanctified loot from some enterprising merchant voyage.

Architectural historians emphasize the not altogether successful fusion of Gambello's original ideas with Coducci's completion of the interior, but the *tout ensemble* of San Zaccaria makes it one of the city's most visually rewarding churches. There is always, thank heaven, enough light in which to enjoy its pictures, though you need to select your position carefully so as to receive the full impact of its greatest treasure, Giovanni Bellini's *Virgin and Child with Saints*, painted in 1506, but only installed here, above the first left-hand altar, in the eighteenth century, when certain adjustments had to be made to the canvas.

This is one of these works which draws the onlooker so deeply into its world of shapes and colours that you will find it exceedingly hard to tear yourself away: after more than a decade of visits to Venice, I keep coming back to this particular Bellinian spring for refreshment. The Madonna sits amid a company of saints, Catherine, Jerome, Lucy and Peter, their faces gravely contemplative, while at their feet sits an angel playing a viol, one of those innumerable instances in Venetian painting of La Serenissima's ardent love of music. The colours, with their luminous glow which seems both to borrow something from the daylight within the church and to add a sheen to it, are matched in beauty by the sense of decor in the marble columns and the glass altar lamp, painted to form part of the *mise-en-scène*.

Supposing you are able to focus on anything else for a moment, it is worth walking round the ambulatory (one of whose chapels contains a small late-eighteenth-century organ) to the chapel of San Tarasio, where you can enter the crypt. This chapel, adorned with three superbly gilded mediaeval altarpieces, holds some remarkable frescoes by Andrea del Castagno (1409–1477) and Francesco da Faenza (d. 1451) which represent some of the earliest surviving examples of the Florentine Renaissance spirit in painting to have reached Venice. Signed by the artists in 1442, they portray the Evangelists and various saints in a style of relaxed, uncompromising naturalism. We know nothing about Francesco, and about Andrea his earliest biographer, the Tuscan painter Giorgio Vasari in his *Lives of the Artists*, is wildly inaccurate, accusing him of having murdered a friend of whose painterly talents he was jealous. The story seems the more unlikely as Andrea maintained a highly successful career in Florence, but a certain fierceness in his character is perhaps suggested by what Bernard Berenson calls his 'tendency to communicate at any cost the feeling of power', and the almost aggressive confidence of these images at San Zaccaria rather reinforces the impression.

From Campo San Zaccaria, follow Salizzada San Provolo to the second right turn and walk down Calle della Chiesa to the disused eighteenth-century church of San Giovanni in Oleo, whence a further right turn off the oddly shaped *campo* will bring you out into the little open space in front of the Palazzo Querini Stampalia. The Querini were a great patrician clan, one of whose branches made the political miscalculation of supporting Bajamonte Tiepolo in his 1310 revolt against the senate. In exile they took possession of the Greek island of Astypalaea, in the Dodecanese, whence the 'Stampalia', to distinguish them from other Querini lines.

When the last of the family died in 1869, his palace and its entire contents, including a library of 150,000 volumes, passed to the city, and the picture gallery, spread out among the state rooms on the second floor, is now a museum, all the more attractive because so few tourists ever seem to have stumbled across it. This seems odder in view of the treasures it contains: while the collection as a whole may not rank among the most outstanding in Italy, it offers you a more intimate glimpse than in other galleries of the characteristic Venetianness of Venetian art.

Among its more arresting canvases is the set of sixty-nine views by Gabriele Bella (exact dates unknown) of life in the city during the mid-eighteenth century. These are robustly primitive scenes, employing a lot of blue, red and brown, showing such typical moments as a grand senatorial procession, a smart patrician wedding, a boxing match and – not altogether as rare as you might imagine – a hard winter when the whole lagoon froze over. Later on, among rooms containing the always slightly uncomfortable-looking walnut and rosewood 'parade' furniture of the Venetian nobility, you will discover an early Bellini, *Presentation in the Temple*, still strongly influenced in colouring and design by Andrea Mantegna (1431–1506) and an unmistakably Florentine *Madonna and Child* in a circular frame (art history calls this a *tondo*, meaning round) by Lorenzo di Credi (d. 1537). He was a pupil of the Tuscan master Andrea Verrocchio (1436–1488) and followed him to Venice to help in work on the Colleoni statue at San Giovanni e Paolo (see page 87).

On the other side of the palace, which invariably seems to be the sunnier, we plunge straight into the sumptuous brocades, stuccoed ceilings and lacquer chinoiserie of the eighteenth century, embodied at its most ceremonious by four grand full-length portraits of red-robed procurators. The best of these is by Giambattista Tiepolo, dated around 1754, shortly after the painter came home from Germany, where he carried out what is often seen as his masterpiece in fresco painting, the series of lavishly decorated rooms and great staircase ceiling of the Prince Bishop's Residence at Wurzburg. After that heroic achievement, it must have seemed the easiest thing in the world for Tiepolo, who rarely painted portraits, to oblige Giovanni Querini with a likeness, but his genius was too free-ranging for mere flattery, and the result is a triumph of perceptiveness, capturing, under the foam-like curls of the white periwig, the air of gloomy cynicism and restless discontent in the scornful patrician stare. Its companions, among them a cheerful likeness by Alessandro Longhi (1753–1813) with its sitter's slightly porcine family nose clearly delineated, seem positively demure beside it.

Longhi was the competent son of a far more inspired father. What Pietro Longhi (1702–1785) lacked in technique (his figures are essentially marionettes, each with the same round, doll-like face) he made up for with a remarkably shrewd eye for social detail in dozens of enchanting little glimpses of Venetian life in which we can almost hear the singsong rasp of his characters' dialect and catch the drift of their conversation. The Querini Stampalia Museum has a room full of such genre scenes, a visit to the peepshow, duck-shooting on the lagoon, a noble daughter at her geography lesson, masked figures picking each other up at the Ridotto, the Sagredo family in gala costume. Doubtless Longhi was indulgent towards his subjects, but whatever the family pride of the Venetians, they had and still have a grand sense of fun, so must surely have enjoyed the seasoning of harmless mockery with which the painter drew them for posterity in their less ceremonious moods.

Outside the palace, a lopsided passage leads you through into Campo Santa Maria Formosa, a big square bounded on the left by a *fondamenta* and a canal, and surrounded by an array of superb palaces, a small history, as it were, of Venetian architecture. The Palazzo Vitturi, at no. 5246, belongs to the early Middle Ages, with Byzantine touches in the windows and decorative panels; Palazzo Doria opposite has typical fifteenth-century pointed arches, while Palazzo Priuli, at the far end of the *campo* facing you, reflects the classicizing taste of a hundred years later.

This is one of the pleasantest *campi* in the city for savouring the ordinary atmosphere of day-to-day life, if only because something always seems to be going on here. An old man sells useful household gadgets, children run little stalls full of old comics, there are occasional rallies for the various political parties and a deal of toing and froing by shoppers heading towards the more populous streets nearby. Yet somehow the square manages to retain its own sort of tranquillity, owing in part to the grave old church of Santa Maria Formosa itself, standing in one corner, at a slight angle to the prevailing lines of the broad open space.

The church was founded in the seventh century and takes its

name from a vision of the Madonna, who appeared to Saint Magnus of Oderzo, a local bishop, in the form of a *formosa matrona*, a beautiful matron. The original plan is probably echoed in the present building, designed in 1492 by Mauro Coducci as a set of small cupolas around a central dome. The attractive Baroque belltower was completed in 1688 and carries an odd leering mask above the door at its foot, which Ruskin inevitably seized upon as an image of the bestial corruption of all that was finest in Venetian art.

An Austrian bomb hit the main dome during the Great War, so that the interior of the church has a slightly dingy, inauthentic, cobbled-together quality to it, which robs the altars and chapels of any real atmosphere. It is one of the few ecclesiastical buildings in the city which does not induce you to remain there for a moment or two of prayer and contemplation. There are, however, two or three good pictures: a Greek icon called the Madonna of Lepanto, brought here after playing its part in gaining Venice the great victory over the Turks in 1575, a powerful triptych by Bartolomeo Vivarini (1432–1499) showing the Virgin sheltering a group of kneeling donors under her cloak, and altarpiece portraying Saint Barbara, flanked by Saints Sebastian and Anthony Abbot, the work of Palma Vecchio.

This painter, who died in 1528 (the father, naturally enough, of Palma Giovane who created the ceiling of San Zulian), is the great unsung master in the annals of Venetian art, largely through being overshadowed by his contemporaries Bellini and Giorgione. The Saint Barbara altarpiece has nonetheless received its fair share of praise, especially for the majesty of its dominant female form, robed in brown with a crimson cloak and wearing a diadem. George Eliot called this 'an almost unique presentation of a hero woman . . . with the expression of a mind filled with serious conviction', and she does indeed remind you of Dorothea Brooke in *Middlemarch* or Dinah Morris in *Adam Bede*.

Saint Barbara is the patron saint of gunners (her torturers were struck dead by fire from heaven) and the Italian word for a powder magazine is *una santabarbara*. The Venetian guild of the

Bombardieri worshipped here, but so too did the makers of dower-chests, the Casselleri (their street, Casseleria, is on the other side of the canal). On the 2nd February 944, when some young girls had arrived at the church of San Pietro in Castello to get married, taking their dower-chests with them, a boatload of pirates carried the brides off. The Doge himself, Pietro Candiano II, gave chase, the girls were brought home, and when he summoned the bravest fighters to congratulate them, these all turned out to be cabinetmakers. As their sole reward they asked the Doge to visit their church of Santa Maria Formosa every year on Candlemas day. He received by tradition two gilt straw hats to keep his head dry, two flasks of malmsey to quench his thirst and two oranges to stay his hunger.

Leaving the square at the opposite end from which you entered, walk along Calle di Borgoloco, passing on your right the imposing bulk of Palazzo Marcello Pindemonte Papadopoli, whose seventeenth-century façade is probably the work of Baldassare Longhena. Cross the bridge from Campo Santa Marina (the church here was pulled down in 1820), go along Calle Castelli, turn right, then pause for a moment to enjoy your first sight of one of Venice's most perfect buildings.

The church of Santa Maria dei Miracoli always seems the more beautiful for its dramatic combination of structural economy with decorative profusion. Begun in 1481 to celebrate a miraculous image of the Blessed Virgin, and covered all over with marble, white, grey and yellow, it was designed by Pietro Lombardo to create an illusion of magnificence through the subtle positioning of its windows and columns and the use on the façade of patterning in varied forms cut out of porphyry and green serpentine.

Within, the exotic contrast of one rare marble with another ravishes the eye, but so too does the lively carving on the pillars of choir gallery, the ceiling of carved and gilded panels, the statues above the balustrading on either side of the sanctuary and the enchanting little reliefs of seamonsters and faces framed in leaves, set at the foot of the principal arch. Once upon a time Giovanni Bellini's *Annunciation* adorned the organ doors, but these are now at the Accademia Gallery, the organ is gone as well, and the visitor's sense of awe at this Renaissance harmony is not necessarily enhanced by the piped religious music which accompanies a walk round the church.

Admiring the effect of the canal which sweeps around the western side of Santa Maria dei Miracoli, follow the *fondamenta*, which leads round into a long straight street ending in a bridge over a broad waterway, the Rio dei Mendicanti, ultimately debouching into the lagoon. You have now emerged in front of that striking ensemble which makes up the Campo San Giovanni e Paolo, or, as the Venetians used to call it, San Zanipolo.

To your right stands the shamelessly consequential, overweeningly elaborate Scuola Grande di San Marco. The *scuole*, which formed such an important feature of life in old Venice, were confraternities devoted to charitable works and caring for the welfare of their members' families, under the patronage of various saints. This one, founded in 1260 and numbering many of the richest patricians in its brotherhood, was given its present façade in 1485 by Pietro Lombardo and Mauro Coducci, though it was Sansovino who enlarged the building in 1533. Doubtless there is something a little vulgar, to the eye in search of pure lines and unadorned surfaces, in all the marble panelling, fussy little cornices and beadings, pilasters, crockets and perspective reliefs of scenes from Saint Mark's life, but to an unprejudiced onlooker with some sense of Venetian decor the whole achievement has an irresistible confidence about it.

The building is now the central hospital, and it is not uncommon to see funeral launches setting out from here for the short trip across the lagoon to the cemetery island of San Michele. Looking down upon death, or on the lively scamper of children playing in the *campo* (there are always a handful – Ruskin once tried to stop them chipping bits off the Scuola and nearly got lynched for his pains), is the unflinchingly stern figure of Bartolomeo Colleoni, one of the doughtiest of those *condottieri* (soldiers of fortune) who played such a crucial role in the military affairs of early Renaissance Italy.

Colleoni died in immense prosperity at his castle of Malpaga in eastern Lombardy, and understandably requested in his will that the Venetian state, which he had served faithfully for most of his distinguished career, and to whom he had bequeathed his considerable fortune, would raise a statue to him in Saint Mark's Square. This was of course entirely contrary to the political principle at the heart of the Republican government, and there was in any case no question of a public memorial to any individual in the symbolic forum of Piazza San Marco, but a compromise was eventually reached whereby the equestrian effigy might be placed in the Campo San Giovanni e Paolo.

The commission for the bronze figure of the armoured Colleoni astride his warhorse was finally assigned to the Florentine sculptor Andrea del Cione, known as Verrocchio (1436–1488), who modelled the charger on what he called 'a natural horse of the streets' and arrived in Venice in 1481 to complete the work *in situ*. At his death it was still at the modelling stage, and the final carving and casting was accomplished by the Venetian Alessandro Leopardi, who signed his name on the girth.

The finished achievement was the ancestor of a whole stable of mounted riders in public places all over Europe, yet its powerful evocation of horse and horseman, not merely as individual man and animal, but also as a fighting unit emblematic of the tougher political realities of Renaissance Italy, makes it perhaps the greatest equestrian statue ever conceived. Vasari tells us that Verrocchio, having heard that the senate planned to offer the work to another sculptor, smashed the horse's head and legs and returned disgruntled to Florence. When an official warning followed that he would lose his own head if he ever set foot again in the Republic's territories, Verrocchio coolly informed the Venetians that they would be foolish to execute him, since his head, so replete with talent and intelligence, was irreplaceable. On the other hand he could always make them a newer and better horse. The Doge and the Grand Council gracefully accepted his point.

Thomas Coryate called the statue 'a goodly Colossus' and drew attention to the punning – or as it is called in heraldry 'canting'

– coat of arms sported by the *condottiere*. Colleoni sounds remarkably similar to the Italian word for testicles, '*coglioni*', and there
indeed on the shield you will see the three 'stones', as the Jacobean
traveller called them – the one extra was presumably intended to
reinforce the notion of the warrior's virile potency.

When Coryate was here in 1611, the *campo* was literally a green
field, which must have offered a still more delightful setting than
it does today for the church which gives it a name. San Giovanni
e Paolo occupies a characteristic position in the city, considering
its original purpose. The rivalry between the two main preaching
orders of friars, the Franciscans and the Dominicans, meant that
they tended to build their religious houses as far from each other
as limited space allowed within the large towns whence they
operated. Even today, in reformed Protestant England, a memory
of this is preserved in places called Greyfriars and Blackfriars at
either end of historic cities. In Venice the followers of Saint
Francis occupied Santa Maria Gloriosa dei Frari, on the Dorsoduro, while those of Saint Dominic settled here, dedicating their
church to two Roman martyrs of the third century.

Doubtless the Frari is better furnished with choice works by
superior hands, but I prefer San Giovanni e Paolo because there
are always fewer people crowding through it (very often you are
almost alone) and it is much easier to enjoy its exceptional synthesis of painting and monuments from the greatest epochs of
Venetian art. The simple structure of the Gothic church, begun
around 1250 but only consecrated in 1430, helps you to relish
these things: a lofty nave and sanctuary culminate in an apse lit
by tall windows pointing slender fingers of light into the building, whose principal walls are braced by wooden crossbeams.

The sides of the nave are lined with an extraordinary collection
of funerary sculpture, some of the finest in Italy and an inspiration
to visiting artists of which echoes can be found in even the
humblest parish churches throughout Europe. Such profusion is
due partly to the building's role as a burial place for successive
doges, for whose lying-in-state it was invariably used. The entire
wall at the western end by which you enter, for example, is

covered by three memorials to Mocenigo doges, two of them, to left and right of the doorway, works of exceptional quality by Pietro Lombardo and his brother Tullio, dating from 1476 and 1500 respectively. An earlier, slightly less smoothly finished achievement of Pietro's is the tomb halfway up the left aisle, of Doge Niccolò Marcello, created around 1475. You can follow the development of the sculptor's style to its earliest strainings away from the Gothic into the Renaissance idiom by seeking out the canopied tomb of Doge Pasquale Malipiero, a little further along on the same side.

Forsaking sculpture and turning left at the top of the north aisle, you enter the Cappella del Rosario, a large, well-lit room which once housed a *scuola* dedicated to the Madonna of the Rosary, on whose feast in 1575 the battle of Lepanto took place. Much ravaged by a fire in 1867, the chapel was restored to its former beauty by the installation of three ceiling panels by Paolo Veronese, rescued from a suppressed church. An *Annunciation, Assumption* and *Adoration of the Shepherds*, they show the artist at his most radiant and assertive, a virtuoso in this specialized field of Renaissance decorative art.

The little scenes from the blessed Virgin's life around the chapel walls are by Piazzetta, shown to splendid advantage in the south aisle of the main church, where the grandly gilt and stuccoed Cappella del Sacramento boasts a tumultuous fresco of 1727, showing *The Glory of Saint Dominic*. The Spanish founder of the Dominican Order performs an airborne homage to the Madonna amid a crowd of angels and adoring friars.

Elsewhere in the church, look out for Lorenzo Lotto's *Saint Antoninus Giving Alms*, above an altar in the south transept. Lotto (1480–1556) was one of his age's most powerfully individual artistic personalities, born in Bergamo, trained in Venice, but ending his life in some hardship among the small towns of the Marche district, further south along the Adriatic coast. In this painting, a mature work of 1542, the tiered structure leads us upwards from a crowd of beggars to two tonsured priests, and

above these the enthroned figure of the saint attended by whisper-
ing angels.

Perhaps the oddest of all monuments in San Giovanni e Paolo's
rich collection stands a little further down the south aisle from
the Cappella del Sacramento. It is in essence a family mausoleum,
thrust, in all its unabashed self-importance, among the sweeter,
more delicate exemplars of funerary art, by the pride of the
Valier family during the early years of the eighteenth century.
Tremendous allegories flank equally monstrous lifesize figures of
Doge Bertuccio Valier, his son Doge Silvestro and Silvestro's
wife Elisabetta Querini. The sculptor Giovanni Bonazza has
caught something of the Dogaressa's notorious ambition and
drive for power. She outraged Venetian convention by having a
medal struck with her likeness engraved, and is said to have
caused her husband's fatal heart-attack during a violent domestic
quarrel. In all its gloomy frittering of artistic resource and pompous flourishes of decorative illusion, there is a certain ghastly
impressiveness about this gigantic confection, completed in 1708
by Andrea Tirali.

Where Silvestro Valier's end was merely pathetic, the last hours
of Marcantonio Bragadin, commemorated by a sarcophagus and
a bust (probably by a pupil of Alessandro Vittoria) at the end of
the south aisle, were genuinely heroic. The gallant defender of
Famagusta, Venice's last stronghold against the Turkish invasion
of Cyprus in 1571, he was forced to surrender the keys of the
garrison to the victorious Pasha, who received him with apparent
courtesy before having his attendant officers carried away to
execution and subjecting him to a lingering torture and death.
First of all Bragadin's ears were cut off and he was made to carry
baskets of earth to the gun-batteries. Then he was tied to a ship's
yard-arm, to be taunted by the sailors. Last and worst was a slow
process of flaying alive, in the presence of the Pasha, during
which the wretched Marcantonio was lucky enough to die. His
skin was stuffed with straw and borne in triumph to Constantinople at the Pasha's masthead. Stolen by a Venetian captive, it was

returned to the Bragadin family and now lies in the sarcophagus here at San Zanipolo.

The Bragadin palace stands in the street known as Barbaria delle Tole, leading out of the *campo* to the right of the church. This name has something to do with carpentry, though experts cannot agree on precisely what. There are still joiners and wood-workers hereabouts, and it is good to inhale the smell of resin and pine-shavings as you thread the sultry *calli* on a summer morning. On your left, as you wander down the Barbaria, is Baldassare Longhena's bizarre musclebound façade (1674) of the church of the Ospedaletto, badly in need of cleaning. This insti-tution, founded in 1527, combined an orphanage and an infirm-ary, but was most popular with eighteenth-century visitors as one of four Venetian 'hospitals' which taught music to their orphan inmates, gathering them into orchestras with high pro-fessional standards, supervised by the leading composers of the day. Charles Burney, who visited the Ospedaletto in 1770, enjoyed the performance of a *Salve Regina* by the orchestra's director, the internationally renowned opera composer Andrea Sacchini (1730–1786), though he noted that in all the orphanages handclapping applause was forbidden. 'They cough, hem and blow their noses to express admiration.'

At the bottom of the street, follow Calle del Caffetier, cross the oblong *campo*, and taking Calle Zen at its southern end, cross the bridge, passing the former church of Santa Giustina, where the Doge used to give specially minted coins to the nuns on the anniversary of Lepanto. Round the back of the building (now a school) you enter Calle San Francesco, which brings you out in front of the Renaissance church of San Francesco della Vigna.

The vineyard in question belonged to Marco Ziani, who left it to the Franciscans in 1253. This is the second church on the site, built in 1534 to a design by Sansovino, though the austerely handsome façade is the work of Andrea Palladio, added in 1568. San Francesco always feels curiously lonely and remote, a little like the Gesuiti only more forlorn. Its tall campanile is one of the strongest punctuation marks across the Venetian skyline. Inside, the effect is hardly striking and there is a certain overall air of neglect, but the church contains several arresting works of art.

On the right as you enter is a fine triptych of three severe-looking saints, Jerome, Bernard and Louis, by Antonio Vivarini. In the left aisle another saintly trio, this time carved in stone by Alessandro Vittoria in 1565, reflects a sturdily Michelangelesque influence. The adjacent chapel has a beautiful late-Baroque decorative scheme in gold, white and grey, with astonishing monochrome figures painted in the vault spandrels by Giambattista Tiepolo. Next to it in the Giustiniani Chapel is a sumptuous Veronese altarpiece, featuring Saint Catherine with her wheel and Saint Anthony accompanied by his traditional black pig, a painting in which the artist's incomparable colour sense is superbly balanced against the sculptural grandeur of the individual figures.

For me the most interesting picture in the church hangs above an altar in the south transept. Almost nothing seems to be known about Antonio da Negroponte, except that he flourished during the latter half of the fifteenth century. 'Negroponte' was the Venetian name for the Greek island of Euboea, so perhaps he was a refugee to Venice after the Republic lost this territory to the Turks. There is very little specifically Greek about his *Virgin and Child Enthroned* here at San Francesco, but the picture is most winning in its colourful, rather amateurish, almost infantine fusion of mediaeval with classical, a solemnly posed Madonna amid bas-reliefs and little ogival aedicules and a great fruit-and-flower garland crowning everything.

Leaving San Francesco della Vigna you can now prepare to enjoy a ramble in this little-known corner of Venice, which, though it preserves the same homely, unpretending atmosphere as Cannaregio, always seems a shade more welcoming and attractive to the eye. Behind the church, follow the Calle del Cimitero into the Campo della Celestia, cross the canal and turn left along Calle Dona. This brings you out into Calle Magno, dominated by a grave old fifteenth-century palace, where you turn down the Calle delle Muneghette ('the little nuns') to follow the *fondamenta* along the canal.

Over the bridge at the end stands the small church of San Martino, one of the humbler, less frequently visited Venetian churches, but not without charm, especially in its baroque false perspectives and in two paintings by Bellini's pupil Girolamo da Santacroce (d. 1556). One of these is a vivid *Last Supper*, painted on the central panel of the organ gallery, the other is a small *Resurrection* above the third altar on the right.

Almost immediately opposite the church is the main gate of the Arsenal, a vital institution in the life of Venice as an independent maritime power. The word 'arsenal', which other European languages assimilated in its Venetian form, derives from the Arabic '*dar sina'a*', 'house of work', which is what this massive fortified enclosure always was until the end of the Great War in 1918. Here, in a complex of shipyards, ropewalks and dock basins, some sixteen thousand men worked on the great galleys of the Venetian Republic, a sight which impressed the poet Dante, who visited the city on an embassy from Ravenna in 1321. The feverish activity of the various artisans, making oars, fitting sails and rudders, and boiling pitch for caulking the timbers, was too good to ignore as an image for inclusion in his great three-part poem *The Divine Comedy*, and was put to excellent use in his description of that part of Hell reserved for the busy traffickers in the sale of public offices.

Another visitor to Venice, the young King Henri III of France, was brought here one morning in 1574 to watch the first stages of a ship in the making: that evening, so it is said, he was shown the same vessel fully rigged and lying at anchor in the dock basin. Perhaps the most famous galley of all built here was the Doge's own processional craft, the colossal *Bucintoro*, or as English travellers always called it, 'the Bucentaur', a name whose origins are clouded in obscurity. As one model succeeded another, the great boat, with its galleries and high poop deck, became more purely ornamental and decidedly unseaworthy. By 1777, the sardonic Dr John Moore, remarking on the wealth of its gilded carving, noted that the Bucentaur 'may possibly be admired by landsmen, but will not much charm a seaman's eye, being a heavy, broad-bottomed machine, which draws little water, and consequently may be easily overset in a gale of wind'. The husband of his contemporary, Anna Lady Miller, described it as 'the ugliest, most tawdry, most contrived vessel he ever saw, loaded with ornaments and gilding, and totally void of grace'.

Its significance in Venice's symbolic reality as a spiritual and political concept was, however, immense. Every year on the Feast of the Ascension, La Festa della Sensa, the Bucentaur, carrying the Doge, the senators, the papal nuncio and the patriarch, 'to the tune of trumpets and the musick of the voyces which sing chearfull Hymeneal tunes' and surrounded by innumerable gondolas, which for this one day in the year were allowed to shed their customary black, was rowed into the lagoon, where the Doge then performed the solemn rite of the Sposalizio del Mar. This was the privilege granted by Pope Alexander III to the Venetians of declaring their dominion over the Adriatic through an annual marriage ceremony (*sposalizio*) where a ring was cast into the sea. The Festa della Sensa is still a holiday in Venice, though the relationship between the city and her native element is nowadays more like that of a divorced couple who sometimes get back together again to chat about old times and enjoy a spot of fun.

Napoleon, almost insanely determined to humiliate the defeated Republic, ordered the last Bucentaur to be stripped and turned into a prison hulk. Some of its myriad ornaments are in the Correr Museum, others now turn up all over the world. You will find a model of it, together with decorative features such as lamps and figureheads from other galleys, in the Museo Storico Navale, a comprehensive museum of maritime history, in front of the Arsenal's eastern wall, at the end of the *fondamenta* where the canal emerges into the Bacino di San Marco. Here also are wondrous ancient maps, Tintoretto's portraits of sea captains and memorabilia from Venice's various successful naval actions, notably the defence of Corfu against the Turks in 1715 and the bombardment of the North African corsair fleets during 1784–85 by Admiral Angelo Emo. He was the Republic's last great hero, a gallant, resourceful, highly cultivated man, who gathered a team of enthusiastic young officers around him to overhaul the Venetian fleet and re-establish, for a few more glorious years, Venice's claim to be the Bride of the Adriatic. His statue, by Antonio Canova, stands in the first room on the ground floor of the museum.

Seadogs of an older vintage are somewhat bizarrely recalled by one of the four lions guarding the Arsenal's main entrance, the tall classical portico built by Antonio Gambello (d. 1481) in 1460. These animals, whatever their allusions to Saint Mark, derive from pagan Greece: one at least is recognizable as coming from the shrine of Apollo on the island of Delos. The two on either side of the gateway were brought from Athens by the campaigning Doge Francesco Morosini 'the Peloponnesiac', after his successful Greek foray of 1687 (it was one of his guns which, in blowing up the Turkish powder magazine in the Parthenon, brought Phidias's splendid frieze crashing to the ground, for Lord Elgin a century or so later to gather up and transport to London). On the left-hand lion you can faintly trace a Scandinavian runic inscription, which reads 'Haakon, with Asmund, Ulf and Orn, conquered this port [Piraeus]. These, with Harold the Tall, exacted large fines from the rebellious Greeks. Dalk is still in distant lands. Egil and Ragnar waged war in Roumania and Armenia.'

This is neither more nor less than an eleventh-century Viking graffito, cut by members of the Byzantine Emperor's Varangian Guard. The name which stands out is undoubtedly 'Harold the Tall', for he is Harald Hardrada, hero of the stirring Norse saga recounting his Mediterranean wanderings, who died in 1066 at the battle of Stamford Bridge, that delusive prelude to disaster at Hastings. The victorious Saxon king Harold Godwinson promised him 'six feet of English earth' and was as good as his word.

From the Arsenal northwards spreads a mixed district, essentially a suburb, neither entirely within Venice nor absolutely outside it, built over what were once fields, orchards and marshlands. Space does not allow me to give you a detailed itinerary, and there is indeed very little here which the traveller interested only in works of art and historic buildings is likely to seek out, but the whole area does possess its own marked character, a sort of village Venice, with more washing lines and cats and pottering domesticity and people calling after each other down the street than you will find around the centre of the town.

Two churches here are worth hunting out. By taking the *vaporetto* number I as far as Sant'Elena, you can reach the pretty Gothic church of that name, built in 1435 on what was once a much smaller island by the monks of the Olivetan order, whose former monastery stands next door. Saint Helen herself, mother of the Emperor Constantine, who discovered the whereabouts of Christ's Cross in a dream, lies in a modern sarcophagus inside the church, an austerely attractive building adorned with an early Renaissance porch by Antonio Rizzo. In the lunette he placed the powerfully-sculpted figure of Admiral Vettor Cappello kneeling before the saint.

A time-honoured custom attached to Sant'Elena was the serving, on Ascension Day, of a meal consisting solely of chestnuts and water to the patriarch of Venice. Amid all the trumpets and junketing, it was intended as a reminder that the saints and hermits of the early Christian church had lived on the humblest possible fare. Traditions of an altogether different kind were linked with the church of San Pietro di Castello, which you will find on its island at the very edge of the Arsenal's northern boundary wall. It was regularly used as a sort of marriage market, from the days when the *casselleri* of Santa Maria Formosa rescued the brides captured here right up to the Rebublic's fall. The prospective wives would appear dressed in white with their dowers in boxes slung over the shoulder by a ribbon, the bishop preached a sermon, the eager young men chose their partners, and that, after the appropriate benediction, was that.

The bishop's presence is significant, for until 1807 San Pietro di Castello was the cathedral church of Venice, its bishop the city's patriarch, while Saint Mark's was, as it were, merely a grand palace chapel. It may indeed be that this remote island, once known as Olivolo before the fort was built which gave a name to the whole *sestiere*, is the oldest settled area in the lagoon. The present church, lofty and august, is the work of Andrea Palladio, begun in 1596, though the façade, which looks so quintessentially Palladian in its classical language of pilasters and pediments, is actually by his pupil Francesco Smeraldi (dates unknown).

Within, much of the best decorative works belongs to the seventeenth and eighteenth centuries. The formidable high altar, for example, was the creation of Baldassare Longhena in 1649, and the ceiling frescoes, by Girolamo Pellegrini (d. 1674), are of the same period. In the first chapel on the left is a vigorously designed *Virgin and Child with Penitent Souls*, by the Neapolitan master Luca Giordana (1632–1705). Known as 'Luca fa presto' – 'Luke does it quickly' – he was one of the most prolific and highly-rated painters of his age, who arrived in Venice in 1685, during the course of successful travels throughout Europe.

On the right chancel wall, a large painting by Antonio Bellucci (1654–1727), who later worked as a fresco artist for English noblemen in London, shows Saint Lorenzo Giustinian imploring God to free Venice from the plague of 1447. Giustinian, who died in 1456 and lies in a sarcophagus on the high altar, was almost the only homegrown saint in a city which needed to import its holy relics as merchandise or booty from the East. As Venice's first patriarch, he is unlikely to have thought well of a governmental system which so obviously marginalized Mother Church's authority, keeping the cathedral firmly on this suburban island, far from the focus of power at Saint Mark's.

If you choose to return towards central Venice along the edge of the lagoon, then your walk will lead you past the gardens whose pavilions every two years house the famous – or as some might say, notorious – exhibition of contemporary art known as the Biennale. Begun in 1895, this has become one of the most highly-rated showcases for modern painters, sculptors and architects, but like all such omnium-gatherum affairs, it is seldom without its scandals and surprises. Some noted critic always contrives to give offence, some world-renowned artist storms out in a typhoon-sized huff, and the Biennale's profile becomes, as a result, still more sharply defined, though critics of its unchallenged status among world art festivals are surprisingly numerous.

Once you have passed the naval church of San Biagio and the maritime museum beside it, cross the bridge to the broad Riva Ca'di Dio. The large building on your right looks like a crenellated Gothic palace but is in fact a late mediaeval bakery, where loaves and biscuits were produced for Venetian garrisons and ship's crews. Over the next bridge you regain the Riva degli Schiavoni, where a right turn at Calle del Dose brings you into what was until quite recently one of the more atmospheric among the quiet *campi* and *campielli* of Venice.

I say 'what was' because the agreeably reticent air of Campo Bandiera e Moro has lately been disturbed by the imposition, on its southern side, of a bar and a restaurant, something it really does not need. Try to come here therefore early in the morning, or late at night when there is nothing to disturb its slightly melancholy gravity.

The dominant elements are a church (of which more presently), the majestic fifteenth-century Palazzo Gritti Badoer (now a hotel) with its unmistakable arched windows on the *piano nobile*, and almost next to this the Palazzo Soderini, where a marble tablet commemorates the heroes after whom this square is named. Like many heroes, however, Attilio and Emilio Bandiera and their friend Domenico Moro were hopelessly naive and foolhardy. In 1844, having failed to win Venetian support for their subversive anti-Austrian movement known as 'Esperia', they set off south into the Kingdom of Naples to raise a revolt in Calabria and were rounded up and shot for their pains. English readers may care to ponder the fact that it was Her Majesty's consular agents who were instrumental in betraying the whole scheme to the Austrians and Neapolitans.

Once the *campo* took its name from the church in the northern corner, San Giovanni in Bragora. Nobody seems to know precisely what a *bragora* is or was, though the Venetian word *bragola*, a market square, sounds similar enough to provide a plausible origin. Certainly the church is one of Venice's oldest, founded during the ninth century to house relics of its patron Saint John the Baptist, rebuilt in its present Gothic style between 1475 and 1494, and somewhat unprofitably muddled with during the early eighteenth century.

In the second chapel on the right, in a Rococo marble sarcophagus, lies the body of Saint John the Almsgiver, a remarkable patriarch of Alexandria, who died in 619 after devoting the last years of his life to bringing social justice to the humblest and poorest elements of the community. Besides being boundlessly generous, he possessed great natural charm, a quality we do not necessarily expect to find in saints. Once, noticing that during long services members of the congregation periodically wandered out to talk with one another on the church steps, he abandoned all ceremony and went to join them for a chat. To the scandalized clergy who asked what on earth he thought he was doing, John answered, 'But don't you understand, my children, that the shepherd must join his flock?' His remains were brought here in 1247, though whether purchased or stolen I cannot discover.

Above the high altar, within a carved marble frame, is the lovely Baptism of Christ by Giovanni Battista Cima, known as Cima da Conegliano (1459–1518) from his birthplace in the hill town north of Venice. Of all those who felt the influence of Giovanni Bellini, Cima had perhaps the most poetic imagination, and here there is a pervasive air of nostalgia for his native countryside, with the distant Dolomites, a cloudy sky, ducks on the water, a ferryman, a rider and a shepherd peopling the verdant landscape which provides so rich a contrast for the rite being celebrated in the foreground. On the north side of the chancel hangs another work by Cima, painted in 1502, *Constantine and Saint Helen with the True Cross*, containing an allusion to a disaster which shook Conegliano in the previous year, when a tower collapsed on top of the mayor's palace.

I always leave the Bragora and its *campo* with regret, though the delights of walking in this quarter of Venice are considerable, especially after nightfall, when the dramatic quality of the street lighting gives an additional glamour to everything and the silence of the *calli* and canals is interrupted only by the scurrying of cats and the plop of a rat into the water. On your daytime wanderings, follow the Salizzada Sant' Antonin, passing the rather dull Baroque church of that name, which contains another looted saint, Saba, brought from Acre in the Holy Land by Doge Lorenzo Tiepolo to be his family's patron. Turn right, and at the end of the *fondamenta* you will find the Scuola di San Giorgio degli Schiavoni, which houses three of the most captivating of all Italian pictorial cycles, the scenes from the lives of the saints by Vettor Carpaccio (1456–1525).

At the same time that Cima was working on his second painting for San Giovanni in Bragora, Carpaccio received his commission from a confraternity of Dalmatian merchants to decorate their *scuola* with celebrations of their three patrons, Saint George, Saint Tryphon and Saint Jerome. From the brio and wealth of narrative detail in these paintings, which used to adorn the upper hall but now hang in the darker ground-floor room, it is obvious that the artist revelled in his task, perhaps also because he was working for a less conventionally sophisticated clientele than native Venetians would have provided. Successive generations have shared Carpaccio's joy in the smallest of details, the animals and birds which occasionally threaten to steal the scene, the little touches of exotic Orientalism – palm trees, a parrot, a monkey, the gaily-clad throng of turbanned Turkish musicians – the curious bystanders, the townscapes melting into delicious Veneto prospects. Of all the world's painters, he is one of the most gifted storytellers, holding our rapt attention at such moments as Saint George's furious gallop to save the princess from the dragon or the headlong flight of the terrified monks before Saint Jerome's tame lion.

Yet even this talent, so prodigally indulged here, in what Ruskin called 'a little room about the size of a commercial parlour in an English inn', did not hinder Carpaccio from creating one of the most moving images in art of dignified stillness and con-templation. The last of the Saint Jerome cycle in fact shows Saint Augustine sitting in his study, quietly reading one of his friend's letters. Sunlight streaks into the room indicating the moment when a miraculous voice told Augustine that Jerome was dead, and a little dog looks up towards a table strewn with scholarly books. Henry James wrote admiringly that the picture 'unites the most masterly finish with a kind of universal largeness of feeling, and he who has it all in his memory will never hear the name of Carpaccio without a throb of almost personal affection'.

The canal outside the *scuola* is called the Rio di San Lorenzo, and though the huge, barn-like church of that name, burial place of Marco Polo, is nowadays only ever opened for occasional exhibitions, it is worth recalling that this was one of Venice's most notorious convents. If things at San Zaccaria were fairly relaxed, matters at San Lorenzo were ordered in an even more accommodating fashion. Few of the nuns, after all, had any real vocation, since most of them were parked here by patrician families, unable or unwilling to find suitable husbands. The *parlatorio*, where they were allowed to talk to visitors and of which Francesco Guardi has left a raffish image in a famous painting, was a place of gossip, flirtation and assignation. Many nuns had lovers, some had children, and, all things considered, life in the cloister for a well-heeled noble girl was far from mortifying or repressive.

Instead of crossing the bridge outside the Scuola di San Giorgio, walk back along the *fondamenta* to the next bridge, where the Salizzada dei Greci leads you to the Greek church, also dedicated to Saint George. Venetian links with the Greek world extended beyond the ambivalent Byzantine connection, and the presence of refugees from Constantinople after its fall to the Turks, of fugitives from Epirus and the Morea, and of Venice's colonial subjects from Crete, Cyprus and the Ionian islands, created a strong Hellenic community, which in 1539 was able to build its own church, designed by Sante Lombardo (1504–1560) and completed by other hands in 1561.

The beauty of its dark, solemn interior, with candle flames and little lamps casting fitful gleams upon icons, marbles and mosaics, derives from the simple fact that the place is not intensively trampled over by tourists and that people do not come here, as to other churches in the city, to gape at works of art. The smell of wax and incense and the glimmer of gold on the iconostasis make this one of the most spiritually charged places in a town where it is all too easy to ignore holiness except as a showcase for some painter's masterpiece, triple-starred in a guidebook. If, on the other hand, you are only after icons, then the Hellenic Institute next door to the church boasts a wonderful collection, many of them seventeenth-century Cretan and pervaded by various Venetian stylistic touches.

The lane behind San Giorgio dei Greci joins a narrow *calle* which takes you back onto the Riva degli Schiavoni, and as you emerge into the full glare of daylight, there stands the church of the Pietà, or, as it is officially called, Santa Maria della Visitazione. With its fine white marble façade, based on a design by the eighteenth-century architect Massari but only added in 1906, this makes an ideal conclusion to a day spent exploring the Castello district, but since it is usually open only in the late afternoon, you should see it as a prelude to an early-evening drink rather than as an aperitif before a long lunch. I am certainly playing devil's advocate here, having formerly expressed pious regrets as to the role of churches as consecrated museums, but the visual effect of the Pietà is indeed a wonderful tonic to the most jaded of sightseers. Massari's interior, completed in 1745, relies on bright light rather than the customary religious gloom as a means of celebrating the Virgin to whom the building is dedicated, and the oval design, together with graceful choir galleries, marble altars and a pulpit on slender gilt legs, contributes to an overall buoyancy and elegance, sublimely rounded off by Giambattista Tiepolo's *Triumph of Faith*, splashed with negligent ease across the ceiling.

The church served the most important of the four musical orphanages referred to earlier, the Ospedale della Pietà, originally founded as a home for abandoned babies in 1346 by Fra Petruccio di Assisi, and placed under the protection of both the Doge and the Pope. This charity still exists in a modified form, but its great days were undoubtedly during the eighteenth century, when the orchestra of girl virtuosi achieved international fame. Husbands would ultimately be found for most of them, but meanwhile they learned to excel on every instrument from the viola d'amore and the tromba marina (a sort of double bass, despite its name meaning 'marine trumpet') to the chalumeau (an ancestor of the clarinet) and the serpent.

To gain the post of music master at a Venetian orphanage was the ambition of all Italian composers, and the Pietà in this respect was especially fortunate in acquiring the services of the great Antonio Vivaldi (1675–1741). Born and baptized in the next-door parish of San Giovanni in Bragora, he had taken minor orders as a priest, but lived openly with his mistress, a singer named Anna Girò, and led a busy life as an opera composer and theatrical impresario in addition to his official duties directing concerts at the Pietà.

Far from being the creator of 'easy listening' musical wallpaper in the form of those much-abused Four Seasons concertos, Vivaldi was a truly original genius, devising his own unique sound-world and planting the roots of a musical style which influenced

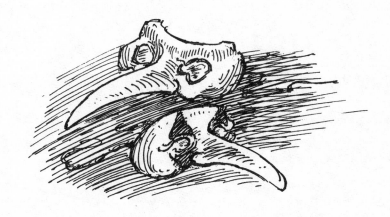

the whole of Europe. He could not have achieved this quite so powerfully without the help and inspiration of the brilliant orphan girls at the Pietà, for whom he wrote some five hundred concertos, sonatas and vocal pieces. Alas, the 'Red Priest', as he was known from his ginger hair, was incurably restless and kept coming and going from his work at the orphanage, lured all over Italy and across the Alps by the promise of yet more success. When he died, it was not in Venice, but at Vienna, where the music-obsessed Emperor Charles VI 'talked to him more often in fifteen days than he speaks to his ministers in two years'.

5 : Painters' Venice

Italians, those born connoisseurs of gastronomy, rarely if ever have a good word to say about Venetian food. Italy itself is famous for the excellence of its 'poor' cookery, in which brilliant results are achieved by the imaginative use of those basic resources available to the peasants of the various regions. The Veneto was never an especially prosperous area, but the early introduction of maize, known as *granoturco* ('Turkish corn' though it originally came from America), produced a staple foodstuff for its humble farming communities in the shape of *polenta*, a sort of yellow porridge eaten in steaming dollops or else hardened and cut up into slices. This accompanied, and still accompanies, most meat and fish dishes, and you will find it useful to acquire a taste for it early in your encounters with Venetian cuisine.

Perhaps ironically, the most interesting dishes here come from

Venice's mainland satellites, such as Padua, Verona and Bergamo. Venice itself, we are assured by historians, was once celebrated for its sophisticated eating and drinking – was it not here, after all, that the use of the dinner napkin and table fork was first introduced? Nowadays, however, the picture is frankly depressing: tourism was already gnawing at the heart of Venetian cooking before fast food came on the scene in the 1980s. There is something genuinely ominous in the presence of burger bars, with their ranch-style furnishings and plastic fascia, in the centre of the city, not just because of their incongruous vulgarity among Gothic palaces and Renaissance churches, but because of what they tell you about the low expectations of modern tourism and about the terrifying readiness of commercial Venice to destroy the very place whose attractions it aims to sell.

Once upon a time it was altogether different. The nineteenth-century writer John Addington Symonds, whose ardent enthusiasm for the city was partly the result of a long and passionate relationship with a handsome gondolier named Angelo Fusato, describes a visit to a Venetian restaurant. 'It is a quaint, low-built, unpretending little place, near a bridge, with a garden hard by which sends a cataract of honeysuckles sunward over a too-jealous wall . . . Our way lies under yonder arch, and up the narrow alley into a paved court. Here are oleanders in pots, and plants of Japanese spindle-wood in tubs; and from the walls beneath the window hang cages of all sorts of birds – a talking parrot, a whistling blackbird, goldfinches, canaries, linnets.'

After patting the restaurant's dog Athos and stroking 'that ancient grey cat, who has no discoverable name, but is famous for the sprightliness and grace with which she bears her eighteen years', Symonds walks into the kitchen to greet the owner and his cook. 'Here we have the privilege of inspecting the larder – fish of various sorts, meat, vegetables, several kinds of birds, pigeons, thrushes, ortolans, geese, wild ducks, chickens, woodcock, according to the season . . . There can be no difference of opinion about the excellence of the cuisine, or about the reasonable charges of this *trattoria*.'

Places of this kind have more or less disappeared in Venice. Apart from the fact that it is no longer possible, unless you know the management very well indeed, to stroll into the kitchen and select your meal from the slab, as it were (apart also from the fact that you will not find thrushes and ortolans on the menu), the charges are unlikely to be very reasonable. Given the low standards of service and the uninspiring menus offered by so many Venetian establishments, the mark-up in comparison with similar places on the mainland, showing a good deal more civility and culinary initiative, often appears frankly outrageous.

If you are lucky enough to stumble across one of the small handful of decent restaurants, you will soon realize that the rest of Italy has been unnecessarily disparaging on the subject of Venetian cooking. Though a regional speciality is *risotto* in various tempting incarnations, you should try the pasta dishes, such as nettle pie, spaghetti with cuttlefish and, in winter particularly, *pasta e fasoi*, a sort of bean purée with vegetables and small crescent-shaped *maccheroni*. A favourite of mine is *bigoli in salsa*, a type of spaghetti accompanied by a sauce of anchovies and onions. Don't miss the duck and guinea fowl in the savoury sauce known as *peverada*, and never scorn the *fegato alla veneziana*, that simplest but most delectable way of preparing tender, paper-thin slices of calf's liver. As for fish, the lagoon, by some environmental miracle, goes on yielding its harvest of mullet, snapper, John Dory, eel and the rest, to be eaten grilled or fried in oil, without the foppery of sauces or condiments which would surely be used to disguise them elsewhere.

Time out of mind, the market for all these good things of the table has been established under and around the arcades on the west side of the Rialto Bridge. After the failure of Bajamonte Tiepolo's plot in 1310, the Venetian state confiscated a palace here belonging to the Querini family, implicated in the conspiracy, and vengefully turned it into a slaughterhouse, or, as the Elizabethan traveller Fynes Moryson refers to it, 'a shambles'. The fish market, as he tells us, 'lies by this shambles, a great length along the banke of the great channell, and in the same shambles and fish market . . . great plenty of victualls, especially of fish, is daily to be sold'. All along the lanes, from the foot of the bridge, the busy stalls of the fishmongers, butchers, green-grocers and cheese-vendors keep up their trade, following a tra-dition unbroken for purely practical reasons since the Middle Ages. The fruit and vegetable barges still unload their mainland cargoes here, as they did in 1783 when William Beckford, early one morning, watched young patricians pausing to nibble at a pear or a peach before going home to sleep off a night's frenetic revelry.

To your right, as you leave the bridge, stands the starkly beautiful early-sixteenth-century Palazzo dei Camerlenghi, designed as a combination of government offices with a small prison, and beyond this is the little church of San Giacomo di Rialto, Venice's oldest religious foundation, from the very earliest days of settlement on the islands of the lagoon. The projecting portico of columns under a sloping roof is a unique survival from these primitive beginnings, as is the ground plan of the church itself, unchanged even though the present fabric dates largely from rebuilding in 1531 and 1601.

Though San Giacomo is hardly ever open, you may be lucky enough to catch a glimpse of the interior, with its dome and apses and Grecian marble pillars and altars venerated by the guild of the grain-winnowers (garbeladori) and that of the goldsmiths (orefici). Bread and jewellery are two commodities still sold around the Rialto. The church and its big fifteenth-century clock on the façade stand somewhat uncomfortably amongst all this huckstering and moneychanging, though some may see it as the perfect image of Venice's easy juxtaposition of business with religion.

Outside market hours, however, this is the least attractive area of central Venice, smelly, squalid and extremely dark at night. Those who dislike crowds will want to move on quickly, so follow the street in front of you, Ruga di Speziali (the spice merchants), cross the next campo, and at the end of the calle you will emerge beside the church of San Cassiano, a mediaeval

building much refurbished during the seventeenth century. Though this is not an especially attractive interior, with its dusty red velvet hangings and chunks of late baroque and rococo decoration looking like cold leftovers from a ceremonial banquet, it does contain one splendid canvas by Tintoretto, a Crucifixion dating from 1568. Instead of offering us the scene in its usual panoramic presentation, with Christ at the dead centre of the composition, the artist created one of his boldest and most dramatic works by placing the crucified Jesus and his accompanying thieves at a sharp sideways angle on the picture's right-hand edge. The dominant element is not Jesus but the diagonal line formed by the Virgin and Saint John in the lower left-hand corner, pointing to two men climbing a ladder to fix the mocking 'I.N.R.I.' inscription to the head of the cross, while the background fairly bristles with menacing halberds and spears. This painting, together with a comparably fine *Resurrection with Saints Cassian and Cecilia* by the same artist, hangs beside the high altar. Cassian, incidentally, is the patron saint of teachers – wrongly, in my view, since he was a savage disciplinarian, appropriately martyred by his long-suffering pupils, who stabbed him to death with their pens.

Outside the church, cross the *campo* and follow the street to your left into Calle della Regina, named after Caterina Cornaro Queen of Cyprus, whose substantial palace stands to your right, with its façade opening onto the Grand Canal. This is a pleasant little quarter of small shops, restaurants and such cheerful touches of Venetian domestic life as trilling cagebirds and bright shows of potted geraniums on the windowsills. Once upon a time it was given over to more specialized delights, as an area swarming with prostitutes and as the site of the first Venetian opera house. The famous courtesans of Venice were not any old daughters of joy, plying their trade at the street corners, but often highly sophisticated women whose skills in the arts of love were matched by learning and artistic versatility which made them more like Japanese geishas than their sisters in other European cities. Their business was of course carefully regulated by the state, which maintained a dozen naval galleys out of the tax they paid, but it seems that Venetian husbands saw them as a kind of safety valve, indirectly protecting their wives from too much philandering. Thomas Coryate grew quite wide-eyed on the whole theme of the courtesans – 'so infinite are the allurements of these amorous Calypsoes, that the fame of them hath drawn many to Venice from some of the remotest parts of Christendome, to contemplate their beauties and enjoy their pleasing dalliances' – though he did advise his readers, were they to visit a harlot's house, to pay up quickly, otherwise she might have you arrested for debt or even murdered by hired bravoes.

It was in this parish of San Cassiano that during the early seventeenth century one of the first of the world's opera houses was opened for public performance. Opera had been 'invented' in Florence, but it was in Venice that the new form really found a home as an exciting new entertainment, with Claudio Monteverdi and Francesco Cavalli as its most outstanding pioneers. In their wake followed a host of less talented but equally popular composers, using libretti combining serious stories from myth or history with elements of farce, pantomime and pure scenic spectacle. Evelyn, watching Giovanni Rovetta's *Ercole in Lidia* in 1645, marvelled at the 'variety of scenes painted and contrived with no less art of perspective, and machines for flying in the air, and other wonderful notions; taken together, it is one of the most magnificent and expensive diversions the wit of man can invent'. The French traveller Limojon de St Didier thought the 'Machines . . . sometimes passable and often ridiculous' and poured scorn on the ballets, as well as finding it quite absurd that the gondoliers should be allowed to shout appreciative comments on the women singers up on the stage.

At the bottom of Calle della Regina, a broad street takes you up to a charming old *campo*, lined with mediaeval palaces, surrounding the church of Santa Maria Mater Domini. This is another of those rarely opened Venetian churches, whose design presents an interesting fusion between the Lombard manner popular in the city during the early sixteenth century and the more assertive idiom of Jacopo Sansovino, who assisted with its completion in 1540. The building's formal compactness makes an agreeable setting for the painting of *Saint Christina Rescued by Angels*, a mature work by Vincenzo Catena (1470–1531), a spice merchant who learned to paint as a pastime, from no less a master than Giovanni Bellini. No wonder Hugh Honour, author of the best Venetian guidebook, is moved by the sophistication and confidence of Catena's work to call him 'the first and greatest amateur in the history of art'.

Following the street opposite the entrance to the church and turning slightly to your left at the end, you reach the entrance to Ca'Pesaro, the city's museum of modern art and most impressive in its own right as an example of the conspicuous expense which a patrician family might still be capable of during the early period of Venice's economic decline in the seventeenth century. 'Money no object' was evidently the guiding principle for the local branch of the Pesaro clan, grown rich from their ownership of a carrier's business and so known as Pesaro del Carro, who commissioned Baldassare Longhena to design them the grandest imaginable *palazzo*. Beginning with the courtyard loggias around 1660, and concluded, at some stage before 1710, with the powerful rusticated frontage overlooking the Grand Canal, the scheme was nevertheless bedevilled by lack of funds. The total impression is that of a somewhat forbidding grandeur, as though the family were standing rather too ponderously on the pedestal of its dignity. Your eye feels the strain of the deeply-incised windows, the heavy keystones like petrified cauliflowers, and the awkward accretions of statuary above the window arches and over the portico.

The last of the palace's owners, an art-loving Piedmontese general named Giuseppe La Masa and his wife Felicita Bevilacqua, presented it to the city as part of a foundation designed to help struggling painters and sculptors, and the building now houses a collection of nineteenth- and twentieth-century art, providing a handsome exhibition space for shows linked to the Biennale. Though the display is international, the stress here is on Italian and particularly on Venetian painters, and these include one of my personal favourites, Ippolito Caffi (1809–1866), last of the great *vedutisti* in the tradition of Guardi and Canaletto. Caffi, who also worked in Rome and travelled in the East, brought a singular delicacy of touch to his views of Venice under the Austrians, against whom he fought in the 1848–9 revolution (his campaign notebooks, illustrated with vivid little sketches of life in the front line, are in the Correr Museum). Alas, it was another struggle with Austria which killed him, when the ship on which he served at the naval battle of Lissa was torpedoed.

Immediately opposite the courtyard entrance of the palace is Calle Pesaro, at the top of which a right turn leads you round into the highly theatrical Campo San Stae, presenting the church of that name to admiring passengers up and down the Grand Canal which washes the square's marble steps. San Stae is a Venetian contraction of 'Sant'Eustachio', another recherché dedication in this city of lesser-known saints. Like Saint Hubert and Saint Julian, Saint Eustace, martyred during the reign of the Emperor Trajan, had a vision of the crucified Christ while out hunting (the Saviour appeared between the antlers of a stag), but I am not sure why the Venetians should have found him so attractive a saint unless, like certain of their tutelary figures, it was because he was popular with the Greeks.

Recent restoration has unveiled San Stae as one of the loveliest Baroque churches in Italy. Like San Vidal, in Campo Santo Stefano, it was paid for by a doge's legacy. When Alvise Mocenigo died in 1709, after a comparatively short reign of some ten years, he left provision in his will for a church to be built close to his family's palace, which stands to the east of it. The chief architect was Domenico Rossi, assisted by a team of sculptors including Antonio Corradini (1668–1752), whose international fame brought commissions from Dresden and Prague, and his father-in-law, Antonio Tarsia (1663–1739), who later worked for Peter the Great in Russia.

Rossi's façade to San Stae takes the standard Palladian form of tall columns topped by a sharply-delineated entablature with a

triangular pediment above, and plays upon this with a wealth of ornament which, so far from spoiling the overall power of the design, acts rather like a set of airy musical variations on a sturdy original theme. Saints pose on pedestals within niches or loll gracefully along the declining angles of the broken pediment over the door, allegories guard the topmost parapets, and there are finely moulded relief panels to punctuate the discourse of Corinthian columns which gives the whole construction its basic strength.

The same confident Baroque tone prevails within, where the Mocenigo family vault is marked by a Doge's horn-shaped cap set in stone in the floor of the nave, with a Latin inscription sombrely declaring, 'The name and the ashes are buried here along with the vanity.' Around spreads the beauty of stucco and marble and altars boasting pictures by the great names of Venice's last splendid artistic sunburst. Here beside the high altar are Giovanni Battista Tiepolo's *Martyrdom of Saint Bartholomew*, Piazzetta's Saint James led to prison, and Saint Peter set free, the work of Sebastiano Ricci (1660–1734), who also painted the chancel ceiling. In the third chapel on the left Jacopo Amigoni (1675–1752) painted the altarpiece of Saint Andrew and Saint Catherine, and in the sacristy Giovanni Battista Pittoni (1687–1767) depicted Trajan ordering Saint Eustace to fight.

Much of the visual pleasure communicated by San Stae derives from the fact that the church was clearly intended as a display case for these painters and their gifted minor followers such as Giustino Menescardi (d. 1776), Antonio Balestra (1666–1740) and Giovanni Battista Mariotti (d. 1743). The whole impression is that of a pictorial 'ministry of all the talents', with certain artists such as Tiepolo and Piazzetta embarking on their careers, and others such as Ricci and Amigoni already established and preparing to set off for foreign shores in search of lucrative new commissions.

Now take the Salizzada San Stae, to the right of the church, and passing the Palazzo Mocenigo, recently opened as a costume museum and worth seeing as a typical patrician interior which has kept many of its eighteenth-century decorative features, turn right into Calle del Tintor. Those with an interest in Venetian history may be interested in the building at the top of Calle del Megio, which leads off this street towards the Grand Canal. This was the granary of the city, where the stores of grain and maize from mainland farms were collected, and you can still see the stone chutes where the corn was tipped out of the hoppers, though the best view of this stolidly functional mediaeval brick construction is from the deck of a Grand Canal *vaporetto*.

In the yellow house by the bridge, opposite the slightly battered-looking Palazzo Priuli Stazio at the lower end of the street (apparently raised to a design by Sansovino), lived Marin Sanudo, a patrician working as a bureaucrat for the Council of Ten, who, until his death in 1536, kept an astonishingly detailed diary, positively Pepysian in its exuberant curiosity, of all he heard and saw in the Venice of his day. The fifty-eight volumes of Sanudo's journal have proved a treasurehouse for everyone from serious scholarly investigators to those simply in search of what it felt like to live in the frenetic, overcrowded city, where gossip and rumour held unchecked sway. Sanudo was fond of a juicy story, from that of the murderess Bernadina, who beat her husband to death, buried his body in the courtyard of their house, and then told friends he had gone as a pilgrim to Loreto, to the tale of the Albanian who bit his wife's nose off as he was taking leave of her before his execution, in revenge for betrayal of him to the authorities as the killer of a certain Zuan Marco. Venice remembers its ebullient chronicler with a Latin inscription on the yellow house overlooking the canal.

Off the zigzagging street on the other side of the bridge, a right turn takes you to the big mediaeval palace known as the Fondaco dei Turchi, from its use during the seventeenth and eighteenth centuries by Turkish merchants, who somehow managed to incorporate within it those three staples of Islamic life, a mosque, a harem and a hammam. The Oriental, or at any rate exotic, appearance of its façade on the Grand Canal is entirely coincidental, and what we in fact see is a modern rebuilding of a

Byzantine palace begun in the thirteenth century for a merchant named Giuseppe Palmieri. In 1381 it was assigned to Niccolo d'Este, Marquis of Ferrara, and in 1435 John Palaeologos, Emperor of Byzantium, stayed here during his fruitless quest for western support against the encroaching Ottomans. By 1850, when the Turks had abandoned the palace, it was in complete decay. 'In contest between life and death', wrote a horrified Ruskin, 'the unsightly heap is festering to its fall.' A drastic and unfeeling restoration turned it into a civic Natural History Museum, probably the least visited of all Venetian collections. Under the long arcade fronting the canal you will find the stone coffin of the wretched Doge Marin Falier, whose skeleton was discovered intact, its decapitated head between the knees, when the sarcophagus lid was lifted five centuries after his execution in 1355.

Beheading is recalled by the name of the nearby church of San Giovanni Decollato, 'San Zan Degola', which means 'Saint John the Headless', referring to the Evangelist's form of martyrdom. This is one of Venice's oldest surviving churches, founded at the beginning of the eleventh century and still retaining its Greek marble columns, several original windows and patches of Byzantine fresco showing the figures of various saints. Like that of San Stefano, the nave is surmounted by a ship's keel ceiling.

Retracing your steps as far as the Fondamenta del Megio, take the right turn which brings you into the big Campo San Giacomo dell'Orio. This grass-grown space has a cheerfully nondescript air about it, a huddle of unassuming houses, shops and restaurants around the mediaeval church dedicated to Saint James. The 'Dell'Orio' part of the name is said to be a corruption of *del lupo*', referring to the wolves which lived on the tiny island where the original church was built, but it is more likely to derive from the laurel tree, *lauro* or *alloro*, which formerly grew there.

San Giacomo dell'Orio has been closed for many years, but if you are fortunate enough to find it open, you will come upon several interesting paintings in the predominantly mediaeval building, including a *Madonna with Saints* by Lorenzo Lotto over the high altar, and a Veronese ceiling in the sacristy. Executed between August and November 1546, the Lotto altarpiece shows how extremely variable in quality the artist's work became during his later years. The saints, Andrew and James, and the medical martyrs Cosmas and Damian, are grouped with singular awkwardness at the foot of a squat, housewifely Virgin under flying putti. Much better is the Veronese *Allegory of Faith*, painted in 1577 for a local *scuola* but, like the Lotto, damaged by neglect and retouching.

Follow the street south of the church, Ruga Bella, into the next *campo*, Nazario Sauro, cross this and walk on until you reach the *fondamenta* along Rio Marin. This is an elegant show of Venetian palace-building at its best, and the pleasure for an interested eye is enhanced by the fact that this long curving embankment, despite its closeness to the tourist-thronged upper reaches of the Grand Canal, is seldom noisy or crowded with passers-by. To your right, on the opposite side, is Palazzo Gradenigo, by Domenico Margutti (1659–1721), and next to this, in the same Baroque style, is Palazzo Cappello, which, like so many other Venetian palaces, passed from one patrician family to another before its interior was substantially gutted during the present century.

At the top of the *fondamenta*, the thoroughfare opens out into a small square in front of the church of San Simeone Profeta, known as San Simon Grande, rebuilt by Margutti along the original mediaeval ground plan during the early eighteenth century. Apart from a heavily restored *Last Supper* by Tintoretto, the real treasure here is the finely carved recumbent figure, on a sarcophagus in the chapel to the left of the high altar, of Simeon himself, shown lying with hands folded and head turned to one side, lapped in the heavy folds of his robe. Neither the provenance of this sculpture, best of its kind in Venice, nor the sculptor himself have ever been established for certain, though an inscription tells us that it was executed in 1317 by a certain Marco Romano. But was he actually working in a Venetian tradition, or did his style derive, as some believe, from the Tuscan workshops of the great Andrea and Nicola Pisano? The beauty of the finished image, with its heavy beard straggling across the breast, the deeply-incised folds of the drapery echoing the crossed hands above them, is incontestable. Here indeed is the spirit of Simeon's own '*Nunc dimittis*' – 'Lord, now lettest thou thy servant depart in peace, according to thy word'.

For San Simon Grande there must be a San Simon Piccolo, though the dedicatee here is not Simeon but Simon the Zealot, yoked, as usual, with Saint Jude. This little church lies up the street (Lunga Chioverette) from Campo San Simon Grande, on the broad *fondamenta* beside the Grand Canal, and has a special significance as the very first image of Venice many travellers receive on emerging from the Santa Lucia railway station. Among Venetian churches it is an oddity, if only because of its singularly bungled attempt at antique grandeur in the design. Over a tall Corinthian portico, the architect Giovanni Scalfurotto (d. 1764) placed a ridiculously disproportionate copper-sheathed dome, in imitation of the Pantheon at Rome, a primitive stab at neo-classicism for Venice by the uncle of the altogether more gifted Tommaso Temanza, creator of the church of the Maddalena.

This is not an especially congenial quarter of the city, crowded as it nearly always is with foot-passengers on their way to and from the car-park and bus-depot of Piazzale Roma, and you are unlikely to linger among the knick-knack stalls and cheap restaurants serving characterless 'Italian' dishes to unsuspecting tourists. Turn left off the *fondamenta*, and follow the side canal until you come face to face with another, far bolder effort to superimpose pagan Greece on Catholic Venice, the church of San Niccolò da Tolentino, originally founded as an oratory in 1528 by the newly-established Theatine Order.

The body of the church itself was built between 1591 and 1602 by Vincenzo Scamozzi. Though Andrea Palladio is said to have had some share in the design, it is more likely that Scamozzi was simply following his master in a somewhat uninspired fashion. The Palladian idiom never died out among Venetian architects – the lasting strength of its impact was reinforced by their pride in the achievements of a local boy – and thus it is hardly surprising to find Andrea Tirali, at the beginning of the eighteenth century, pushing towards a more rigorous interpretation of the great architect's intentions. You will have admired Tirali's noble façade for the church of San Vidal, on the corner of Campo Santo Stefano, but the amazing grandeur of the Corinthian temple porch of tall fluted columns stuck on to Scamozzi's bland San Niccolo dei Tolentini is one of the more entertaining surprises in this corner of the city.

The heavily stuccoed and frescoed interior contains some comparably delightful decorative features. Connoisseurs of funerary art (those, at least, courageous enough to relish Tirali's notorious Valier monument at San Zanipolo) will surely enjoy the tomb, on the left side of the chancel, of Francesco Morosini, who died in 1678 and is commemorated by a most handsome sculptured ensemble by the Genoese master Filippo Parodi (1630–1708). A pupil of Bernini, he devised for Morosini, patriarch of Venice, a dramatic tableau set against a stone curtain imitating the effect of brocade, with flowers on a white ground and a gilt fringe, upheld by flying angels. The mitred patriarch lolls benignly on a tall sarcophagus, with attendant female allegories in swirling robes below. Tirali was clearly influenced by Parodi's work, but there is a more intriguing link here between the ambitious freedom of the whole composition and the spirit of great funerary sculptors such as Michael Rysbrack and Louis-François Roubiliac, working in England during the decades immediately following Parodi's death.

An earlier Genoese who came to Venice in search of a liberal artistic atmosphere was Bernardo Strozzi (1581–1644), a Capuchin friar who absorbed the styles of both Caravaggio and Rubens, eventually quitting both Genoa and his religious order, and dying here as a fugitive from persecution. Strozzi's style is wholly unmistakable: he delighted in painting old, ugly, suffering men, with wattled skin, straggling beards and an abundance of rags. His picture of *The Charity of Saint Lawrence* in the third chapel on the left of the church shows a typically bald, bearded ancient, half naked and turning towards the altogether more shadowy figure of the saint in the background of the canvas.

Turn left outside the church and follow the canal as far as the Salizzada San Pantalon, at the end of which you turn right and cross a *campiello* with one of a dwindling number of Venetian public fountains in its midst. These are not great cascading water-jets in the Roman manner, simply cast-iron columns with open taps from which gushes the sweetest of water. What experience more pleasant than splashing your face with it on a hot afternoon, or, in a sultry midnight where its soft plash is the only audible noise, cupping your hands to receive a blessed mouthful? Alas, like so many good old Venetian institutions, these fountains are steadily being cut off. Enjoy them while you may!

Two canals lap the edge of Campo San Pantalon, on whose north side stands a church, a double dedication to Saint Pantaleon and Saint Juliana, built in the late seventeenth century to replace an earlier mediaeval building. This is one of only a handful of churches in Venice never to have acquired a façade. As at San Marcuola, the brick frontage still awaits its marble completion after three hundred years.

What everyone – everyone with a sense of humour, that is – enjoys inside is the astonishing vaulted ceiling, covered with a colossal painting on canvas by Giannantonio Fumiani (1643–1710), celebrating the life of Saint Pantaleon and his martyrdom under the Emperor Diocletian. Very well, Fumiani was not a great painter, and there is more than a slight sense of overweening fatuity about some of his effects, but the *coup de théâtre* here is utterly breathtaking. The overall design makes unquestionably skilful use of foreshortened figures, as well as creating a surreal dimension involving gigantic allegories, like colossal painted cutouts, who seem to be dragging the edges of the whole turbid compositional jumble into another dimension altogether.

After all this, it is something of a relief to be able to turn to the Chapel of the Holy Nail, on the right side of the church close to the altar, commemorating a sacred relic of the Crucifixion, presented when the nearby convent of the Clarisse was suppressed in 1830. Here you will find a striking *Coronation of the Virgin*, dated 1444, the work of Antonio Vivarini (1415–1476) and his German assistant Giovanni D'Alemagna (d. 1450), known as Zuan Tedesco. Further down on the same side is a late painting by Paolo Veronese, *Saint Pantaleon Healing a Sick Girl*, completed by the artist's son Carletto. Augustus Hare, in his Victorian guide to Venice, mentions both these works, but simply cannot bring himself to utter the name of Fumiani, whom no good Ruskin-imbued aesthete could ever have learned to love.

Following the *calle* to the right of the church and turning right once more, you reach the fifteenth-century Palazzo Corner (a vernacular form of the patrician name Cornaro) and beyond this stretches a broad canal. The bridge across it is called Ponte della Frescada, 'bridge of freshness', because it is the only place in Venice where, whatever the heat or humidity or stillness of the air, you are always likely to find some slight waft of breeze blowing. Even on the sultriest of Venetian afternoons, when the surrounding streets are empty of all save a few sleeping cats sprawled across the hot paving stones, a little gust or two cools your face here as you contemplate a nap after a long lunch.

On the other side of the bridge there is an agreeable canalside walk before the third *calle* on your right brings you out into the narrow open space in front of the church of San Rocco and its adjacent *scuola*. Saint Roch was a French nobleman from Montpellier, who took a vow of poverty and set out on a pilgrimage to Rome. During the journey he devoted himself to tending the sick patients of various hospitals in towns along the way, but on his return, while at Piacenza, he himself caught the plague and was looked after by angels and a faithful dog who brought him food. When he recovered and reached Montpellier, he was so completely unrecognizable that his fellow citizens flung him in gaol, where after five years he died. The warders entering his cell found it flooded with a bright light, and saw an inscription on the wall promising that all plague sufferers who called on his name would be healed.

In the case of Saint Roch, the Venetians in 1485 did exactly as they had done several centuries earlier with the body of Saint Mark. Merchants disguised as pilgrims stole the remains from a church at Montpellier and brought them back to Venice, where a recent pestilence had decimated the population. In response to this plague, a guild of flagellants, known as the Battuti di San Rocco, was founded, and their church, designed by Bartolomeo Bon, had its foundations laid in 1489.

Hardly any of this original building survives. What we see instead is an early-eighteenth-century box by Giovanni Scalfurotto, with a most appealing late rococo façade by Bernardino Macaruzzi (d. 1798) in which frames and niches feature a series of particularly fine statues and reliefs by Giovanni Marchiori (1696–1778), a pupil of the great Andrea Brustolon, and Giovanni Maria Morlaiter (1699–1782), a sculptor of Austrian origin who later worked for Empress Catherine the Great of Russia.

Inside the church, with its decidedly glamorous high altar, created around 1520 by a family of decorative artists from Bergamo named Fantoni to enshrine the sarcophagus of Saint Roch, are several good eighteenth-century paintings, including Sebastiano Ricci's *Saint Francis of Paola Reviving a Dead Baby* (1732) above the first right-hand altar, and a lyrical Annunciation by that most poetic of Neapolitan masters Francesco Solimena (1657–1747) on the opposite side. The pretty ceiling panels in the vestry date from the same period, the work of Francesco Fontebasso, who seems to have spent much of his creative life in a horizontal position under the roofs of churches.

The most important pictures here are those on the walls of the choir, showing scenes from the life of Saint Roch, by Jacopo Tintoretto. It is indeed for Tintoretto that most of us visit San Rocco, but we are less interested in the works he left in the church than in the phenomenal series of canvases with which he adorned the great *scuola* beside it. This Scuola Grande di San Rocco was begun by Bartolemeo Bon in 1516 and finished in 1549 by Antonio Abbondi, known as Lo Scarpagnino (1510–1549). Architecturally it is one of Venice's most interesting late-

Renaissance buildings, the more so because of the somewhat uneasy synthesis between the windows of its lower storey, whose roundels make them curiously reminiscent of Gothic cloister arches, and the heavily-pedimented and pilastered lights of the upper floor, surmounted by a looming entablature along the parapet.

Tintoretto's work for the Scuola di San Rocco commenced in 1564, when the brotherhood of the Battuti invited submissions from various artists, including Paolo Veronese and the Tuscan painter Giuseppe Salviati (1520–1575), for a decorative scheme to adorn the walls and ceilings of the grand saloons. A story which may well be true says that while several candidates worked diligently at their drawings, Tintoretto raced to complete an entire painted panel and, on the day when the commission was to be announced, unveiled it to the fury of his fellow competitors and the admiration of everyone else.

The labour of accomplishing the entire series of panels took the artists some fifteen years, during which the upper and lower halls and their adjacent rooms were covered with a sequence of paintings on scenes from the Old and New Testaments, programmatically connected according to contemporary custom. For example, in the upper Sala Grande, the ceiling pictures, on such themes as Moses Bringing Water from the Rock, The Gathering of Manna and The Feast of the Passover, are directly related, in the *scuola*'s context as a charitable institution, to those around the walls, portraying such moments as The Last Supper, The Miracle of the Loaves and Fishes and Christ at the Pool of Bethesda. The Sala dell'Albergo is dominated by a stupendous Crucifixion, rightly characterized by Ruskin as 'beyond all analogies and above all praise', while the wonderful canvases in the lower hall, arguably this prolific artist's best work, represent moments from the childhood of Christ, flanked by moonlit scenes of meditative saints.

For some time after the fall of the Republic, the destiny of the Scuola di San Rocco lay in the balance, and it looked as if its paintings might be sold and the entire building demolished.

Ruskin, visiting it in 1846, found rainwater dripping through the ceilings. Now, thanks to painstaking restoration, the original brilliance of Tintoretto's conception has been revealed, and we can enjoy to the full his idiosyncratic painterly language of foreshortened figures, deliberately stagy lighting effects, curious geometric tricks with angles, planes and lines, and a palette carefully concentrated on a narrow tonal range. No wonder Ruskin, at his first encounter with his beloved 'Tintoret', grew somewhat hysterical. No wonder, on the other hand, that Henry James thought the Scuola decidedly sinister. 'We shall scarcely find four walls elsewhere that inclose within a like area an equal quantity of genius. The air is thick with it and dense and difficult to breathe; for it was genius that was not happy, inasmuch as it lacked the art to fix itself for ever. It is not immortality that we breathe at the Scuola di San Rocco, but conscious, reluctant mortality.'

You cannot leave the Scuola unmoved, any more than you can enter its immediate neighbour, the great church of Santa Maria Gloriosa dei Frari, without emotion. Though I have to confess that I do not find a visit to the Frari nearly as satisfying as a morning spent in the much quieter and more congenial San Giovanni e Paolo, its correspondent building, I bow to the supremacy of this church as a treasurehouse of some of the best things in Venetian art.

It was the Franciscan order which founded the Frari ('the Friars') in 1250, replacing their earlier church with the present big, austere, brick hangar around 1330. The architect was not, as Giorgio Vasari insists, the Tuscan Nicola Pisano, but most probably a Venetian named Scipione Bon, who, as Fra Pacifico, was a member of the order and is buried within the church, in a tomb in the right transept, decorated with fine terracotta reliefs. For the campanile, the friars turned to Jacopo delle Masegne, whose son Pietro completed it in 1396.

Those who object to being charged admission to churches as a modern evil may like to reflect on the fact that for at least a hundred and fifty years visitors have had to pay to enter the

Frari. A few thousand lire seems very little in exchange for the visual feast which awaits you. So at least thought Anne Thackeray Ritchie, daughter of the author of *Vanity Fair*, arriving here at the close of the nineteenth century, and initially dazed by 'the great church . . . piled arch upon arch, tomb upon tomb', with several of its chief monuments hanging 'high over the heads of the people as they kneel, above the city and its cries, and its circling life, and the steps of the easy-going Venetians'. Like most of us, she seems scarcely to have known where to begin, so bewildering is the variety of artistic experience offered within a single building.

The western end of the Frari, littered with inscribed stones, effigies and sarcophagi, gives you an excellent notion of its gradually assumed role as a sort of Pantheon for distinguished Venetians, born or adopted, along the same lines as San Giovanni e Paolo. At the bottom of the nave on the right is a heavy, glum-looking mausoleum to Titian, commissioned by Emperor Ferdinand I of Austria in 1838 from two former pupils of Canova, Luigi and Pietro Zandomeneghi. Their famous teacher's own memorial, similar in its pyramidal design and completed a decade earlier, stands directly facing it.

Further along on the right, the Zane chapel contains one of Alessandro Vittoria's most expressive works, a Saint Jerome carved around 1570 and, it is said, modelled on the features of the aged Titian himself. Opposite this, over and around the main doorway, is the megalithic tomb of Doge Giovanni Pesaro, one of the shrewdest of Venetian diplomats, who, after stiffening the Republic's resistance to the Turks in the long mid-seventeenth-century struggle for Crete, enjoyed only one year as supreme figurehead before dying in 1659. His memorial is a weird *mélange* of death's-heads and grinning blackamoors by the German sculptor Melchior Barthel (1625–1672), developing an idea by Longhena.

A century and more earlier, another Pesaro, Jacopo, Bishop of Paphos in Cyprus, had led a successful onslaught against a Turkish force attacking the island. In 1519 he ordered from Titian a superb altarpiece, the so-called *Madonna di Ca'Pesaro*, which the young artist took seven years to complete. The result was one of the most captivating of all Venetian religious paintings in its originality of concept and in the assurance with which it celebrates the dignity, honour, piety and wealth of a patrician family. As it hangs before you, to the right-hand side of the main doorway, you can marvel both at the composition's bold diagonal, with the Virgin and her merry little Christ Child gazing down on the kneeling Pesaro donors, and at the richness of Titian's palette, already glowing with that radiance which generations of later painters have coveted (including Sir Joshua Reynolds, whose particular favourite this was among the artist's works).

You are now more or less level with the Friars' Choir, separated from the main body of the church by a tall marble screen, created in 1475 by the great Bon family of sculptors under the direction of Pietro Lombardo, its niches and parapets adorned with images of apostles, prophets and doctors of the church. Within this enclosure are Marco Cozzi's exquisitely designed choir stalls, the finest woodwork of its period in Venice, perhaps in all Italy, dating from 1468, a ravishing sequence of landscapes and perspectives in intarsia work, surmounted by relief panels of saints.

What the choir has effectively hidden from you, unless you have very sharp eyesight, is the triumphant *Assumption of the Blessed Virgin*, painted in 1518 by Titian as his earliest major commission and hanging above the high altar of the central apse chapel. This amazing achievement, conceived in a daring series of ascending layers, is one of the seminal works of European art, stunning in its sense of epic grandeur and in a sort of glorious inevitability which fuels the entire painting, from the group of all too humanly astonished apostles on the lowest level to the heavenward-soaring Madonna, in Bernard Berenson's words, 'borne up by the fullness of life within her, and by the feeling that the universe is naturally her own'.

The sheer force and beauty of Titian's *Assumption* are answered in several different ways by the works of other great Renaissance artists in this part of the church. In the small chapel immediately to the right is a painted wooden statue of John the Baptist, carved by Donatello and brought here from Padua in 1451, an image of raw eloquence which offers a most telling contrast with Jacopo Sansovino's treatment of the same saint on the marble font of the Corner chapel to the left, dating from a century later.

Next to this, under a simple leger stone, lies the composer Claudio Monteverdi (1567–1643), born in Cremona but identified, more than any other musician, with the splendour and freeflowing fancy of late Renaissance Venice. The sound of his motets, 'spiritual concerti' and psalm settings is as quintessentially Venetian as the sensuous discourse of his surviving operas (though the earliest and most famous of these, *Orfeo*, was written for the ducal court at Mantua). His gorgeous *Vespri della Beata Vergine* ('The Vespers of 1610', as they are also known) are sometimes performed at the Frari, soothing doubtless to the spirit of their tirelessly inventive and influential creator.

On the south side of the chancel, in the third chapel on the right, is a *Madonna and Child with Saints* by Bartolomeo Vivarini, a typically colourful and sharply-etched work by an artist whose more famous contemporary and collaborator Giovanni Bellini is represented by an exceptionally lovely triptych above the altar of the adjacent sacristy. Painted in 1488 for a memorial to Francesca Tron Pisani, and still surrounded by its cunningly architectural frame designed to heighten perspective illusion, this calm-eyed Virgin, holding the infant Jesus between her tapering fingers and flanked by a quartet of saints, breathes all that visionary gentleness which we associate with this most influential of the great Venetian masters. So many artists emerge from their biographies as bad-tempered, spiteful old curmudgeons that it is a pleasure to find that Bellini, in the course of a long life, enjoyed teaching, liked painting portraits and loved his family. Such humanity may not necessarily have affected the quality of his work, yet who can ignore the hand of a good man in this Frari triptych?

The conventual buildings which formerly sheltered the Franciscan friars lie on the right of the *campo* behind the church. A double cloister, its parapets decorated with eighteenth-century statues of angels and saints, the Ca'Grande dei Frari now shelters the Archivio dello Stato, one of the world's most fascinating archives by virtue of the wealth and variety of the documents stacked along its corridors. The whole history of the Republic is here, the treaties, the ambassadors' dispatches, the minutes of council meetings, the marriage contracts of noble families, the secret reports of spies and the inventories of private palaces. Every year the Archivio organizes richly detailed exhibitions on different historical themes, selected from its treasury of maps, letters, diaries, illuminated charters, sketchbooks and manuscript jottings, and these will often tell you a great deal more about the way in which La Serenissima actually worked as a city and a state than many a formal history book.

The beauty of the sculptured tombs in the Frari having made its due impact, you may well be in search of further examples of the skill with which artists in stone adorned Venice. One of the more attractive illustrations of the way in which Renaissance builders and carvers could fuse their talents is afforded by the Scuola di San Giovanni Evangelista, which stands almost immediately behind the Archivio dello Stato, across the canal, in the next *campo*. Among the more venerable *scuole* and, like that at San Rocco, a confraternity of flagellants, it was founded in 1261 and moved to the present site in 1454.

Several of the greatest hands in Venetian design worked to create this noble courtyard, these halls and porticoes. Pietro Lombardo made the screen enclosing the court, with its eagle pediment, grey pilasters and delicate leaf-sprays in the frieze, while Mauro Coducci, during the same closing decades of the fifteenth century, devised a superb double staircase under a vaulted roof, sweeping up to a great hall, given a somewhat self-important air by Giorgio Massari's 1727 remodelling, with a ceiling painted by various distinguished Rococo hands. A plan to turn this exquisite building into a museum of Venetian sculpture has long been under discussion, and we must hope that it will be allowed to take proper shape.

If you have left the Frari by its *campo*'s rather noisy south-eastern corner, which adjoins the Campo San Rocco, you should walk straight on until you face the hopelessly dilapidated marble façade of San Toma (where, incidentally, there is a useful *traghetto*, or gondola ferry, to take you across the Grand Canal). Turning left and crossing the bridge, you reach the tall Palazzo Centani, a mediaeval building retaining its original courtyard and open staircase, where on 25th February 1707 that most lovable, fecund and inspired of Italian dramatists Carlo Goldoni was born.

It is a singular fact that practically nobody who has ever had anything memorable to say about Venice has been authentically Venetian by background and ancestry. Goldoni's father was a doctor from Modena, who left to get further qualifications in Rome soon after Carlo's birth, but the boy, growing up in the tattered splendour of the Serene Republic during her last great days, became a truer son of Saint Mark than any native gondolier.

Gifted with an amazing fluency of invention, Goldoni brought the entire eighteenth-century world onto the stage. He is most famous for his comedies of Venetian life, plays such as *Il Campi-ello* and *Il servitore di due padroni*, in which traditional characters from the old *commedia dell'arte* theatre mingle with ordinary people from the streets and squares, all of them talking the dialect you can still hear in the city today. His imagination ranged well beyond Venice itself, however, and some of his most spirited plays, such as *Il ventaglio* and *La locandiera*, are sophisticated vignettes of high life among the provincial aristocracy of Tuscany and Lombardy – though he was careful never to bring a Venetian patrician onto the stage. Through all his work, whether social satire or situation comedy, there runs a vein of melancholy, which mirrors the turns of his career as a dramatist. Not content with Italian success, he was lured to France, where the last thirty years of his long life produced very little of real quality, and where he died impoverished in 1793.

His birthplace now contains a little museum and an institute for dramatic studies. The real Goldoni memorial you will find all around you, in the speech patterns and cadences of the

Venetian accent, in the conversations you hear in shops and restaurants and on the deck of the *vaporetto*, in the casual exchanges between passers-by. It is a tribute, rather than an insult, to some larger-than-life middle-aged woman with a loud voice and a theatrical manner to call her '*veramente goldoniana*', 'straight out of Goldoni' – and there are plenty of such splendid figures still left in Venice.

At the end of the street in front of the palace, turn left and then right (passing Da Ignazio, one of the city's best restaurants). Over the bridge you come upon the broad Campo San Polo, whose Romanesque and Gothic church has been much meddled with during ten centuries and not always for the best. The church's patron, Saint Paul, is represented by one of a pair of dignified bronze statues (his companion is St Anthony the Abbot) on either side of the high altar, by Alessandro Vittoria, dated around 1570. All around the interior is a set of small paintings showing the Stations of the Cross, executed in 1747 by Giando-menico Tiepolo (1727–1804), son of the more famous Giovanni Battista but no mere *fils à papa*, as the French say. His own very personal idiom is interesting to compare, even at this early stage of his career, with his father, who painted the brilliant *Apparition of the Virgin to Saint John Nepomuk* above the second altar on the left. Have a look also at the pretty little Chapel of the Sacrament, off the apse, with its cupola lantern and frescoed ceiling of 1702 by a late Baroque artist named Gioacchino Pozzoli.

The big *campo* outside has been turned over to every kind of use from a football pitch to an open-air ballet stage and the site of the annual Festa dell'Unità, the fund-raising fair for the Italian Communist Party. In 1546 it was the scene of one of the most famous Renaissance murders, the assassination of Lorenzino de'Medici, himself a fugitive from justice after the killing of his cousin, the hated Duke of Florence, Alessandro de'Medici. A high price on his head made him a hotly-pursued quarry. The murderers, having waited several weeks for their chance, finally struck as Lorenzino came out of the church. After a violent struggle, one of them 'gave him a great cut across the head, which split in two pieces'. Three centuries afterwards Alfred de Musset turned the victim's bloodstained life and death into that most thrilling of French Romantic melodramas, *Lorenzaccio* (1834).

The crime must have been watched with appalled fascination by dwellers in that stately cluster of palaces which rings the square. Most of these are of the fifteenth century, with typical tall windows and balconies, pointed late Gothic arches and handsome detailing in carved marble. At the corner of the *campo* furthest from the church, Palazzo Corner Mocenigo once sheltered the bizarre British Venetophile Frederick Rolfe, better known under his pen name of Baron Corvo (1860–1913). Catholicism, homosexuality and paranoia were the significant elements in a life lived perpetually on the margins of society, whether in England or Venice, a city for which he developed a passionate appreciation, partly because, unlike most English expatriates, he spent much of his time here in the company of ordinary Venetians. Getting to know the canals and sailing among the islands of the lagoon, he wrote his masterpiece *The Desire and Pursuit of the Whole*, a novel which is really an extended celebration of the Venetian experience.

Often wretchedly poor, Corvo made life no easier for himself by his unscrupulous scrounging and by a continual readiness to bite the hands that fed him. In 1909 he became the guest of a Doctor Van Someren and his wife, who lived here in Campo San Polo. Earning his keep by doing odd jobs around the *palazzo*, he finished *The Desire and Pursuit of the Whole*, which the Van Somerens were naturally curious to read. Almost as if he wanted them to turn on him so that he could rage at them later on, Corvo showed his hosts the manuscript. When they discovered that it included a ferocious series of satirical portraits of leading figures in the Anglo-Venetian colony, he was asked to leave forthwith. He revenged himself by adding an equally savage pair of caricatures to the novel.

A sadder story than Corvo's comes to mind as you leave the square and walk straight on in the well-signposted direction of the Rialto. Off the Campo Sant'Aponal, in front of the disused church of that name, runs the Calle Bianca Cappello, leading to the Ponte Storto. Bianca was the daughter of a patrician family, who lived in the palace to the left of the bridge. In 1568, aged only fifteen, she met and eloped with a Florentine bank clerk, Pietro Bonaventuri, who took her to his home town, where they married and lived not very happily, while the Serene Republic issued warrants for their arrest. One day Francesco de'Medici, Grand Duke of Tuscany, happening to pass their house, caught sight of the pretty young bride at a window and soon afterwards made her his mistress, having Pietro murdered in the process. When Bianca finally became Grand Duchess, the Venetian Senate, hurriedly changing its tune, hailed her as 'a faithful daughter of Saint Mark'. Hated by the Florentines and ostracized by Francesco's family, she grew peevish and miserable, eventually dying within a few hours of her husband, apparently from the effects of a poisoned pie, though the real cause was probably the imprudent diet the pair had been following. While Francesco was interred with solemn honours in the Medici mausoleum at San Lorenzo, Bianca was unceremoniously dumped in a pauper's grave in the crypt of the same church, and her story endured as a cautionary tale of the fruits of pride and ambition.

From Sant'Aponal, the narrow main thoroughfare which returns you to the Rialto is essentially a busy shopping street, but where it broadens into the Ruga Vecchia you should seize the chance of a look at the small church of San Giovanni Elemosinario (the same Saint John the Almsgiver whose shrine you have already seen at San Giovanni in Bragora). Rebuilt in 1527 after a fire had ravaged this area, it contains a serene Titian altarpiece, painted around 1545, showing the patron saint giving alms to a beggar. In the right-hand chapel nearest the chancel is a panel of three saints, Catherine, Sebastian and Roch, the work of the artist's undeniably talented competitor Giovanni Antonio Sacchiense, known from his birthplace as Pordenone (1484–1539), and the two works make an absorbing comparison. The corresponding chapel on the left side is called the Cappella dei Pollaioli, the poultry sellers' chapel, reminding you that when you step outside it is into the thick of those teeming provender markets at the foot of the Rialto Bridge.

6 : The Surprise of the Salute

Among those who fall in love with Venice, only the luckiest ever get to live there. We are all entitled to our fantasies, however, and most of us, in that dream world in which cravings and ambitions are instantly satisfied, have already selected the ideal *palazzo* in the part of the city most perfectly suited to our moods. The more adventurous will probably choose Cannaregio, where they can live amidst pure-bred Venetians without the possibility of bumping into other expatriates around every corner. Those in search of quiet and remoteness will retire to the solitude of the Giudecca, making occasional rather condescending journeys across to Saint Mark's and the Zattere, if only to reinforce the conviction that distance leads enchantment to the view. Some are justifiably fond of the quarter around the Greek church and San Giovanni in Bragora, and a few eccentric souls go to ground in the farthest reaches of the Castello district, beyond the Biennale gardens.

One area especially has become the favoured haunt of affluent in-comers, living with a certain shyness and simplicity as befits those who combine great wealth with decent measures of taste and discretion. This is the zone stretching from the Ca'Foscari (now the University of Venice) to the church of Santa Maria della Salute, on the extreme tip of the smaller of those two large islands which make up the central portion of the city.

Nobody is quite sure why this region is called the Dorsoduro. One authoritative contemporary guidebook declares that the name means 'hard back', referring to the heavy clay subsoil. Another suggests a corruption of the word '*dosso*', meaning a hillock, of which there were apparently several in what nowadays seems a perfectly flat stretch of terrain, distinguished in any case by other features which give it a certain particularity, an 'apartness' from the tourist-crammed streets and squares on the other side of the canal.

In the most affectionate and incisive of the shorter Venetian guides, Sheila Hale calls Dorsoduro 'the Greenwich Village or Chelsea of Venice, a privileged domestic neighbourhood', and so indeed it is. There are no big noisy thoroughfares, like the Mercerie or the Lista di Spagna, and the canals are not clogged with jostling barges or gondola parties complete with accordion-playing serenaders. There is something benign rather than depressing in this tranquillity and emptiness. Dimensions for enjoying Venice are perfect here because so little clutters the perspectives and you will always find enough space in which to stand back and savour the various effects of light, sound and colour around you.

You notice the change almost as soon as you cross the Ponte Foscari, over the broad arterial waterway linking the Grand Canal at its halfway point to its outlet into the lagoon at Piazzale Roma. To your left as you come over the bridge is the fine fifteenth-century Gothic palace called Ca'Foscari, the name often loosely given to Venice's university, though in fact this houses only one of its faculties, the Istituto di Economia e Commercio. It was here, in 1457, amid what Ruskin poetically calls 'these ruinous and time-stricken walls which tower over the water', that the wretched Doge Francesco Foscari, who had originally bought the site from the Milanese Sforza family, returned to his new-built *palazzo* to die of a broken heart. As a devoted servant of the Republic and her longest-reigning Doge (he was elected in 1423), Francesco might be thought to have deserved a happy old age, but the vengeful fury of the Loredan family, which drove his son Jacopo into lifelong exile on a trumped-up charge, pursued him to the last.

When the young man, allowed a final interview with his family, pleaded with his father to save him, the Doge, as a good Venetian, had sternly answered: 'Oh Jacopo, obey what thy country commands and seek nothing else!' Yet he too, along with Jacopo's wife and children, wept openly, a fact sardonically noted by the Loredan, who instantly adduced this as proof that Francesco was no longer capable of upholding the dignity of his office. The ultimate humiliation arrived for Foscari when he was formally deposed by a vote in the Grand Council and told to quit the Doge's Palace within eight days. The implacable Loredan, unmoved by the news that a member of the Erizzo family had confessed on his deathbed to the murder of which Jacopo was accused, were satisfied only by hearing the bell toll for their ancient enemy, ground down at last by hatred, ingratitude and the inexorable demands of the state he so loyally served.

The Ca'Foscari's sadder associations have long since been purged by its role as a university building. Italian universities are, with one or two shining exceptions, racked with financial corruption and administrative abuses, but Venice remains one of the better schools, especially in such fields as architecture and Oriental languages. Further scholarly activity continues in the two adjacent palaces. Palazzo Giustinian, the nearest of them, sheltered Richard Wagner, who composed the second act of *Tristan und Isolde* here during the winter of 1858–9, closely watched by the Austrian police, who even noted the colour of his bedroom curtains. From the back of the building he could look out upon the pleasant, brick-paved Campiello degli Squellini, with its little grove of plane trees around a fountain. Out of this, a dark, zigzagging lane takes you to the Ponte San Barnaba, where, instead of crossing the bridge, you should follow the *fondamenta* to your left, which leads at last to one of Venice's most sumptuous treats, the uncompromisingly gorgeous palace known as Ca'Rezzonico.

The whole phenomenon of eighteenth-century Venetian life and culture is still something of a puzzle to historians and writers on art. Was not the Republic, after all, on its last legs, economically exhausted after an ultimately fruitless struggle against the Turks? Who on earth took it seriously as a world power? In the end, what was La Serenissima in 1700 but a political fantasy, a charade sustained to shore up the self-importance of its nobles?

It would be easy to leave it at that, but the reality is more complex and fascinating. Imperial powers decline very slowly, and there was still apparently plenty of money for Venetians to spend long after they had lost their Grecian territories to the Ottoman. The patricians turned to the resources of their mainland farms, which yielded enough to sustain a handsome lifestyle for many of them (amid a hugely proliferating nobility, many of whom were redundant to the state's administrative needs), until the arrival of French Revolutionary ideas about liberty and equality heralded the nemesis which fell in 1797 with Napoleon and his Army of Italy.

Others besides the great aristocratic families were able to enjoy life in a city where the pursuit of pleasure was sophisticated almost to the level of an art form. Repressive and eternally suspicious though the Venetian senatorial government was, it knew how to sustain civic loyalty through the cynical expedient of what the Roman emperors used to call 'bread and circuses'. There was always enough to eat and there were plenty of opportunities for celebration, so much indeed that it often seemed as if the Venetian year were one long carnival and that nobody ever went to bed for anything so banal as sleep.

What fun it must have been, that Venice of Vivaldi and Goldoni, of midnight assignations, masquerades, fireworks, processions, freak shows, mountebanks, tumblers, music in churches and palaces, and every season a new crop of operas and star singers at the various theatres, and what a dazzling final burst of artistic creativity sprang from this palace of so-called decadence and decline! The Ca'Rezzonico, taking its name from the *nouveau riche* Genoese banking family who bought and completed it in the early eighteenth century, makes a perfect showcase for the collection of paintings and furniture of the period brought together from various sources after 1935 when the municipality acquired it from the last owner.

The grand scale of the palace is emphasized as you enter through a courtyard with a large watergate to your left, giving onto the Grand Canal. At the top of an ample main staircase, one of several finishing touches added by Giorgio Massari for the Rezzonico during the 1740s, you pass through a sequence of state apartments along the *piano nobile*. First comes a tremendous ballroom, complete with *trompe l'oeil* architecture, tall pedimented doorways, massive gilded chandeliers, and a portentous frescoed ceiling, showing the four quarters of the world, by Giovanni Battista Crosato (1685–1756), one of several talented assistants of Tiepolo who worked in the palaces of the Sardinian royal family in and around Turin.

Here and in the next room are chairs and vase stands by that most inspired of Baroque wood sculptors working in Venice, Andrea Brustolon. With their ornate foliage and fanciful use of blackamoor heads and figures, they have been much copied by makers of reproduction furniture, many of whose shops, displaying various stages of the 'antiquing' process, you will have noticed in the streets of this quarter of Venice. There is evidently a thriving market for such stuff, though the fakers can never hope to reproduce Brustolon's essential panache. Nor has anyone been able adequately to stimulate the combination of fantasy, grandeur and sheer entertainment so professionally displayed in the various rococo frescoed ceilings adorning these noble rooms.

The finest of these are of course by that master of the whole genre, Giovanni Battista Tiepolo. In the first saloon on your right, look up at his *Allegory of Marriage* (1758), where Apollo's chariot carries the newly-wed Ludovico Rezzonico and his bride, Faustina Savorgnan (from one of the 'good old families' of mainland aristocracy), and further on, in the bedroom where the pair spent their wedding night, notice the witty presentation of *Merit Between Nobility and Virtue* as an opening in the roof through which trumpeting putti whirl aloft into the cloudy vault of heaven.

It used to be possible (and perhaps it is once again) to go down from this level to a series of little mezzanine rooms once lived in by Cardinal Rezzonico, elected Pope in 1758 as Clement XIII. It was in these so-called Papal Apartments that the poet Robert Browning spent his last days. He had grown to love Venice and the Veneto as a young man, but only renewed his interest in the city in 1878, when the wealthy American hostess Katharine de Kay Bronson invited him to stay at her *palazzo* on the Grand Canal, Casa Alvisi, and the pair thereafter enjoyed what the French pleasantly term *'une amitié amoureuse'*. Browning started to look for a palace of his own, and it came as a stroke of great good fortune when his son Pen married another American heiress and was able to acquire the Ca'Rezzonico. Though the great Victorian bard only spent a few weeks living here before his death on 12th December 1889, the link between poet and *palazzo* is an apt one, since his *A Toccata of Galuppi's* is generally considered the most perfect distillation of the world of eighteenth-century Venice.

Upstairs again, among the frescoes and guildings and swags and mock architecture, you can luxuriate, as Browning surely did, in imagining these grand saloons as the setting for patrician pomps and junketings. In 1769 the Archduke Joseph, son of Empress Maria Theresa, was serenaded here by the finest girl musicians from the four musical orphanages, surrounded by an audience of six hundred nobles and their gorgeously-attired wives and daughters. As the Emperor Joseph II, he antagonized Pope

143

Clement's successor Pius VI by his high-handed treatment of the Church, and in 1782 the Pontiff actually journeyed from Rome all the way to Vienna to remonstrate. Failing in his purpose, he returned by way of Venice, where he gave audience here in the Throne Room under the splendid canopy and red damask hangings.

On the other side of the large central atrium, the *portego di mezzo*, lies the library, never a specially important element in a Venetian *palazzo*, but fitted up with fine dark mahogany bookcases and a dashing set of ceiling allegories by Francesco Maffei (1625–60). In the adjacent rooms were another gorgeous set of Brustolon furniture, made originally for the Venier family, and a shimmering, feather-light Tiepolo fresco of *Fortitude and Wisdom* from a Barbarigo palace, one of the painter's most idiosyncratic creations.

In the *portego* upstairs a picture gallery gathers together some of the major talents of late Baroque and Rococo Venice, artists who knew by the merest brushstroke how to amuse the city's 'millionaire socialites', as James Lees-Milne in his delightful essay on the Ca'Rezzonico calls its former owners. Here is Giovanni Antonio Pellegrini's *Mucius Scaevola in Porsenna's Camp*, as operatically colourful as Piazzetta's *Death of Darius* seems sombre and menacing. Here are landscapes by Zais, Zuccarelli and Carlevaris, and two vivid and entrancing scenes showing a Ridotto or gaming room in full swing and the parlour of a convent, with masked gallants ogling the nuns behind their grille, the work of the Guardi brothers Giannantonio and Francesco.

What nearly everyone loves best of all at Ca'Rezzonico are the set of little glimpses of Venetian life by Pietro Longhi and the frescoes painted by Giandomenico Tiepolo for his father's country house at Zianigo near the mainland town of Mira. All the witty astuteness of observation which you will have enjoyed in the Longhi collection at the Galleria Querini Stampalia is matched here as we peer once more through these miniature windows into a world which, even though Napoleon and the Austrians swept so much of it away, survives at least in spirit here and there among the *calli* and on the canals. As well as a fashionable levee, a musical evening, visits to a fortune-teller and a doughnut stall, there is a trip into the country, where a peasant woman doles out *polenta*, and a sequence of small portraits, including one purporting to represent an Irish giant called Cornelius Magrath, standing seven feet tall and weighing over fifty stone. Perhaps the latter detail is simply charming Hibernian exaggeration, but we do know that Magrath visited Venice in 1757 and was much admired.

The Tiepolo frescoes, rescued from foreign export in 1910, carry us to another universe altogether. Significantly one of them shows figures looking at a peepshow called the Mondo Novo, but Giandomenico's new world is a haunting one of masked clowns, fantastically-garbed strollers, men and women with their backs firmly turned to the onlooker, all moving towards a romantic Alpine landscape of jagged peaks and fallen fir trees. There is something subversive, even a little terrifying, in the beaky-nosed vizards of the tumbling clowns·and the inexorable facelessness of the walkers and peepshow gazers, as if Giandomenico, for all his sense of humour, were also trying to warn us of the coming reversal of all our comforting assumptions as to the settled order of things.

Once upon a time the Ca'Rezzonico showed visitors to its third floor, which displayed a collection of eighteenth-century costumes, a group of the clay models from which Andrea Brustolon and the sculptor Giovanni Maria Morleiter originally worked, a complete marionette theatre of the period and one of those fascinating old chemist shops of which Venice used to contain several but which thoughtless progress has almost entirely swept away. The world-famous product of these pharmacies was *teriaca*, the 'Venice treacle' supposedly made from something like a hundred different ingredients, including medicinal tree-bark and pulverized fragments of Egyptian mummy. Derived from an ancient recipe, it was also known as *mithridate*, from King Mithridates of Pontus, who had originally devised it as an antidote to all known poisons. The Republic's laws declared that it had to be packed under strict supervision in broad daylight, to avoid tampering and fraud.

You will most likely find the Ca'Rezzonico third floor closed, as it has been for nearly twenty years, though if you are allowed up there you will get several views from its windows of one of the most beautiful roofscapes in Venice, a superb vista across lichen-mottled pink pantiles, mediaeval funnel-shaped chimneys, *altane* (terraces) with potplants and washing lines, and the belfry of a church or two.

Back on ground level outside the palace, you should return along the *fondamenta* to the bridge which carries you over into the attractive Campo San Barnaba, one of the best spots in Venice for lingering over a drink at an outdoor cafe table and watching people come and go. The church of San Barnaba, to your left, is an unremarkable mid-eighteenth-century building, hardly ever open and rendered decidedly scruffy by the growth of weeds and bushes along its topmost parapet. To your right runs a broad canal with barges selling fruit and vegetables, and on the other side of the square is an arch with the words 'Sottoportego del Casin dei Nobili', recalling the area's particular associations during the last decades of the Republic. For San Barnaba was the parish of impoverished nobility, the younger sons of prolific patricians who, for the sake of their nobility, could not work, yet had no interest in performing the administrative offices of state.

The *barnabotti*, as this aristocratic underclass was called from the special lodgings allotted to it here, were a distinct liability. Picking up money from such activities as picture dealing and pimping for wealthy travellers, they were not averse to selling their votes in the grand Council, the only real advantage their high-born status conferred. Perhaps inevitably, they were among the most enthusiastic adherents of the new 'democratic' ideas arriving from France in the wake of the events of 1789, since the preceding decades had witnessed such an unhealthy concentration of political power into the hands of a small number of rich families, and the *barnabotti* saw no reason why they might not now pick up a share for themselves.

Crossing the bridge over the canal, known as Ponte dei Pugni (Bridge of the Firsts) from the stand-up fights which used to take place here between men from the Sestiere di Castello and those of the local Sestiere di San Nicolò, you come gradually round into the big, irregular Campo Santa Margherita, a cheerful, bustling open space named after the extinct church whose remains survive on the northern side, complete with a stump of campanile. Surrounded by shops and cafes, the *campo* features a market selling fish, fruit and kitchen stuff, and several tourist *trattorie*, as well as the Scuola dei Varotari (tanners), the freestanding building facing you as you come in from this side, and boasting a fine carved relief of the Virgin spreading a protective mantle around adoring worshippers.

Walking straight on, past one of Venice's various Chinese restaurants, you arrive at last at the church of Santa Maria del Carmelo, better known as the Carmine, built for the Carmelite friars at some stage during the early fourteenth century. The Gothic structure, much embellished and pulled about in succeeding ages, contains some excellent tomb sculpture, including expressive relief panels on the tomb of Jacopo Foscarini (1602) by an anonymous follower of Sansovino, and a noble female allegory of Virginity by Antonio Corradini, the only survivor from a set of six figures carved in 1721. Apart from the sprightly frescoes in the central cupola by Sebastiano Ricci, the best of the pictures crammed hugger-mugger into every available space are a late Cima da Conegliano above the third altar on the right, showing the Nativity with attendant saints, and a beautiful Lorenzo Lotto of 1529 in the left aisle, in which Saint Lucy and Saint Nicholas are accompanied by John the Baptist and Saint George in the act of slaying the dragon.

Next to the church is the seventeenth-century *scuola*, with its typical arrangement of upper and lower halls. From the latter we mount a fussily stuccoed staircase to the large room on the first floor, where the ceiling is covered by a painting of *The Virgin*

Giving the Scapular to Saint Simon Stock, with four small panels featuring angels in flight. These are the work of Giambattista Tiepolo, completed in 1744 and so much admired by the confraternity of the Scuola del Carmine that the painter was immediately elected a member. Saint Simon Stock was a mediaeval English monk from Cambridge who had a vision of Our Lady giving the Carmelite Order its badge, a simple arrangement of two pieces of white cloth tied by strings over the shoulder (*scapula* in Latin) probably derived from a similar device worn by devout Jews. The main painting is among Tiepolo's finest for its poetic, almost dreamlike treatment of the theme and its use of subtle variations on a carefully limited palette.

The long canal that snakes all the way down from the public gardens opposite the main railway station at the top of Canal Grande almost as far as the open channel between Dorsoduro and the island of Giudecca offers the chance of a pleasant saunter along its quiet banks. On stretches of water like this one, the modern traveller really feels the absence of the gondolas which plied up and down it until changing times and customs put paid to the existence of the graceful swan-necked craft as anything other than a tourist curiosity. Perhaps it was here that the novelist George Meredith in 1861, floating under palace windows, was greeted by 'a very pretty damsel lost in languor' who 'hung with her loose-robed bosom against the iron, and pressed amorously to see me pass, till she could no further'. Telling his gondolier to turn round, he watched entranced as she 'slowly arranged her sweet shape to be seen decently, and so stood, but half a pace in the recess, with one dear hand on one shoulder . . . her drooped eyelids mournfully seeming to say: "No, no, never! tho' I am dying to be wedded to that wish of yours and would stake my soul I have divined it!" – wasn't it charming? This is too so intensely human, from a figure vaporous, but half discernible!'

Cross the bridge opposite the Carmine and follow the *fondamenta*, whence you get a good view of Palazzo Zenobio on the opposite bank, a fine seventeenth-century building which now houses an Armenian college. Almost next door is the pious institution of the Soccorso, a former refuge for fallen women and now a girls' school. Its founder was Veronica Franco (1546–1591), a doctor's wife who became what was known as an 'honest whore', that is to say, a courtesan of the highest rank, and made a certain reputation for herself as a poet.

Many of the Venetian prostitutes of Veronica's day had begun life among poor families from this very area, the quarter of San Nicolò, still one of the city's shabbier districts after many centuries. The Nicolotti, as its inhabitants were called, elected their own Doge, known as the Gastaldo, who, on the day he was chosen, went in procession to Saint Mark's dressed in a wig and a red satin toga to give a fraternal embrace to his grander ducal equivalent.

The delightful church which gave the zone its name, San Nicolò dei Mendicoli (Saint Nicholas of the Beggars) is reached by turning right at the end of the *fondamenta*. The oldest in Venice, it betrays its venerable age by various features, including the Byzantine-style apse at the eastern end and the colonnaded porch which, although dating only from the fifteenth century, echoes the much more ancient porticoes found in various Italian Romanesque churches. Once upon a time this sheltered the poor nuns known as *pinzochere*.

Inside, the building has recently been restored by the English Venice in Peril Fund, so as to emphasize the slightly bizarre effect created by successive attempts to alter the decor without changing the basic shape of the church. The wainscoted panels along the upper nave walls contain paintings of the school of Veronese, and the ceiling, whose beams are left open to view, displays scenes from the life of Saint Nicholas by another of the great painter's followers, Francesco Montemezzano (1540–1602), and by Tintoretto's pupil Leonardo Corona (1561–1605). Veronese's son Carletto Caliari decorated the organ case, and at the end of the nave on the right is a *Resurrection* by the distinguished hand of Palma Giovane.

Cheerful as this interior is, it is worth noting that its survival is nothing short of miraculous. San Nicolò, downgraded from its parochial status in the early nineteenth century, was progressively rifled and despoiled over the next hundred years, though the body in a glass-sided coffin lying in the second chapel along the south aisle was always taken for that of Saint Nicholas himself, that cheerful patron of children and sailors, and reverently left to its mummified repose. Since the saint's bones are generally supposed to have been translated from Asia Minor to the southern Italian city of Bari, it is presumably a case of 'some mistake surely'.

The rather frowzy *campo* outside has a marble column with a lion of Saint Mark on top, who has lost his wings but kept hold of his book. From here, retrace your steps as far as the first bridge over the canal, which will bring you to the church of Angelo Raffaele, standing in a little grass-grown open space looking out over the water. Its towers are among the most distinctive in Venice for their somewhat eastern-European appearance, as if we were halfway down the Danube rather than at the bottom end of a Venetian *rio*. Francesco Contini (dates unknown) built the body of the church in 1618, and the plain façade was added just over a century later, incorporating a Renaissance marble group of the Angel Raphael with Tobias, from an earlier building on the site.

Apart from a spirited ceiling fresco of Saint Michael overcoming the Devil, painted around 1740 by Francesco Fontebasso, and an altarpiece in the first chapel on the left by Giambattista Zelotti (1526–1578), most famous as a fresco painter in the great villas of the *terraferma*, what most people come here to see are the little panels along the organ gallery showing the story of Tobias (in Venetian, 'Tobiolo') by one or other – scholars are still uncertain – of Tiepolo's two brothers-in-law, Francesco and Giannantonio Guardi, dated around 1750. Much better known as a view-painter, Guardi, whichever of them it was, deployed his soft, hazy, yet always so subtly luminous colours here to brilliant effect, and the whole sequence provides one of the most captivating of Venetian experiences, a splendid illustration of the living traditions of painterly fancy and inventiveness during the last decades of the Republic.

From Angelo Raffaele it is but a short step across a sprawling *campo* and around the corner to the church of San Sebastiano, a unique artistic moment in your travels around the city, since its interior decoration is almost exclusively the work of a single great artist, Veronese. Paolo Caliari, who was called 'Il Veronese' from Verona where he was born around 1530, was the last of that astonishing constellation of painters which blazed across sixteenth-century Venice. A less inward-looking master than Tintoretto, he was possessed of a comparably lively and energetic imagination, expressing itself through a palette of gorgeously varied colours, an unrivalled sense of theatricality and a warmly human embrace of the onlooker, as if seeking to draw us companionably into the different scenes, religious, mythological or allegorical, which he portrays. His genius is that of a good man who wants us to share in the joy communicated by a perfect mastery of his craft. Having loved him from my boyhood, I hope that if there is an after-life, we shall meet at last and talk about the wonderful things he made, above all here at the church of San Sebastiano.

Completed in 1545, to a simple design by Antonio Abbondi, Lo Scarpagnino, incorporating a choir gallery running around three sides of the nave, the building became a focus for Veronese's talent at the crucial early, middle and late stages of his prolific and highly successful career. In 1555, his uncle, prior of the Hieronymite order whose monastery this church served, summoned the young man to decorate the sacristy ceiling with a confidently realized *Coronation of the Virgin* surrounded by oblong panels of the Four Evangelists. A year later, he sealed his reputation, which had spread by leaps and bounds among the Venetians, with the ceiling of the central nave, opulently overspread by a masterly trio of scenes from the story of Esther, reflecting the painter's fondness for sumptuous trappings of state, for public spectacle and procession, all of which must have entranced him on arriving from provincial Verona to encounter the mandarin pomps of La Serenissima.

Not content with this, Veronese now embarked on the project of decorating the presbytery, adorning the organ doors with a richly-toned *Presentation in the Temple* and *Pool of Bethesda*, and flanking the high altar by two scenes from the life of Sebastian the soldier martyr, while the central altarpiece shows the Madonna in glory with saints. Besides these lavish outpourings of his inexhaustible imagination and love of the purely decorative and ceremonial, he covered the upper nave walls with an eye-catching frieze of twisted columns framing figures of prophets and sybils. San Sebastiano is not unique as a church given over to the genius of a single artist, but precisely because the painter here is Veronese, it always seems much warmer and friendlier in its embrace of the visitor than any other place of this kind. It is typical of his modesty that his tombstone, in front of the high altar, should be as simple and unostentatious as possible.

A narrow street, aptly named Calle Lunga for its extent, drives straight up from San Sebastiano to San Barnaba, between some unpresuming little *trattorie* and shops. Just before you reach Campo San Barnaba, turn left, cross the canal (Rio Malpaga) and walk along the quiet *fondamenta* beside the still, glassy Rio delle Eremite, where gondolas and other craft lie moored. A little way down is Montin, the most congenial restaurant in Venice for those intelligent tourists who want simply-prepared, flawlessly authentic Venetian dishes served without fuss and nonsense in an atmosphere which reflects the attraction of this Dorsoduro quarter for artists and writers. By a miracle Montin has blessedly resisted commercial blandishments and remains officially what its modest sign proclaims, a *locanda*, a small inn where two or three gravelly-voiced Venetian drinkers are always at the bar by the door, where in summer the tables are set out under a pergola in the back garden, and where the staff are still wonderfully polite and unobtrusive. Having been dogmatic about Veronese, I may as well be equally downright about this place and say that nobody who cares for Venice doesn't keep a small part of that love for Montin.

At the end of the *fondamenta*, turn left, passing some attractive small *palazzi* and getting a glimpse of what remains of the garden of Ca'Michiel, formerly one of the most renowned in a city which – wrongly – we seldom associate with interesting gardens. You come out at last onto the broad *campo* in front of the church of San Trovaso, whose nobly-conceived sixteenth-century south façade, with its plain pediment and tall hemispherical upper window, was the work of an unknown architect clearly inspired by Andrea Palladio's church of Le Zitelle on the island of Giudecca, directly across the lagoon. Next to it stands the campanile of an older building in Romanesque style which collapsed in 1583, when the present San Trovaso was begun. The dedication is another of Venetian scrambled names, like San Stae and San Marcuola, belonging originally to the martyr saints Gervase and Protasus. The fact that the church has another façade, opening onto the *campo* itself, is attributable to its being a sort of neutral territory for the Nicolotti, mentioned earlier, and their rival popular faction the Castellani, who slugged it out annually with each other on the Ponte dei Pugni.

The Clary chapel, in the right transept, is named for the family of Prince Alphonso Clary, who died in 1978, after a long life which had included service in the Austrian Imperial army in the Great War and flight from the Czech communists who seized his Silesian estates in 1945. His remarkable memory and far-spread dynastic connections among the noble houses of Europe made him an infallible resource for historians and biographers, and grateful references to the genealogical expertise of 'Alphy' Clary head many a list of acknowledgments. The chapel altar presents a ravishing example of high Renaissance sculpture in the carving of its panels, a harmony of musical angels framing further angels bearing instruments of Christ's Passion, by an anonymous artist evidently schooled in the most refined traditions of the late-fifteenth-century north Italian style. Two powerfully-drawn

Tintorettos hang in the left transept, a *Last Supper* and a *Jesus Washing the Feet of His Disciples.*

The area around San Trovaso makes a pleasant place to sit and rest, on the church steps, on the canalside parapet, on the benches underneath the trees at the edge of the *campo*, during a hot morning's sightseeing. Alternatively, you could cross the bridge a little way along and walk down the *fondamenta* to get a glimpse of something peculiarly Venetian, though alas almost the last of its

kind. This place is a *squero*, a repair yard for gondolas, at which the black boats are reconditioned, caulked and painted afresh, much as they were a hundred or indeed a thousand years ago. The word *squero* is said to derive from the Greek word *eskharion*, meaning a launching slipway, but some experts take it from a Venetian term for a carpenter's chisel. Other craft besides gondolas, including the characteristic twin-oared *sandalo*, are built or refitted here, and the boatyard never stays idle from one end of the day to the other.

Walking on, you come out at last onto the Zattere, the broad, busy waterside which commands a spectacular view across the Canale della Giudecca, with a ceaseless traffic of big ships, ferry-boats and smaller vessels, and the island of Giudecca beyond, its profile determined by such buildings as the tall mock-castle of the Mulino Stucky, a flour mill built in 1895 by the German architect Ernst Wullekopf, and Palladio's graceful white church of the Redentore. The original *zattere* were rafts bringing loads of wood from the mainland, but today's rafts are securely fastened to mooring poles, covered over with green awnings and carrying fish restaurants and *pizzerie*, where the food, though expensive, is always dependable and much enhanced by the pleasure of watching the toing and froing along the waterfront.

Further along on your left is one of my favourite Venetian baroque façades, a work which brilliantly fuses the grand and the fanciful in its imposing marble ensemble. The church of Santa Maria del Rosario is always known as the Gesuati, from the order of 'poor' Dominicans known by that name (the 'Jesuates' as opposed to the more familiar Jesuits) who built the elegant little oratory of San Gerolamo almost next door. On their suppression in 1668, the parent order of black friars of Saint Dominic assumed control of the convent, and with their immeasurably greater resources were able to raise the present church.

The design is another by the great Giorgio Massari, who adorned the pillared frontage with marvellously attitudinizing full-length figures of Prudence, Justice, Strength and Temper-ance, arrayed for all the world like the heroines of some ornately-staged opera then playing at one of Venice's various theatres: the female warrior, Strength, in buskins, helmet and tucked-up skirt, is surely singing a robust D major aria with *obbligato* trumpet. Inside, opera changes to oratorio of the graceful Venetian sort, with more fine sculpture, this time by Giuseppe Maria Morlaiter, and a tremendous trio of ceiling frescoes by Giambattista Tiepolo, painted between 1737 and 1739, showing the *Institution of the Rosary*, with the Virgin and Child in glory, and two celebrations of Saint Dominic. Of all the artist's works in the city's churches and palaces, this is the most revealing of his true gifts in its buoyant handling of movement and volume and its extraordinary subtlety of tonal emphasis on pinks, greens and greys. In the first chapel on the left you will find another Tiepolo, painted soon afterwards, a Madonna with three female saints, a cheerfully unorthodox composition, while equally attractive 'holy conversations' of distinguished Dominicans by Piazzetta and Sebastiano Ricci adorn chapels further along.

Turn left when you leave the church, and walk up the broad street which used to be a waterway linking the Canale della Giudecca with the Grand Canal. At the foot of the Ponte dell' Accademia, it is worth climbing to the top of the newly-rebuilt wooden bridge for an exhilarating vista up and down the city's great central thoroughfare. Midday here, with the sun glinting on palace fronts and domes and the water thronged with boats, is delightful, whether you turn to admire the high ogival windows of Palazzo Cavalli on your right, the lovely late-fifteenth-century Palazzo Contarini dal Zaffo to your left, or look towards the enchanting little garden in front of the German consulate or the palace opposite which houses the British consul. I recommend a visit to the bridge late at night, when the moon is up, and the shadowy buildings and dramatic lighting effects from high windows and passing boats show you Venice at her most ineffably romantic.

Below the Ponte dell'Accademia, on the side from which you have approached, a profusion of postcard reproductions of paintings, some of them familiar already from art history books, tells you that a gallery is close by. Owing to the weird but apparently immovable Italian law, these souvenir images may not be sold inside museums themselves, though many of the smaller galleries now tacitly infringe this rule.

The Galleria dell'Accademia has never provided the ideal setting in which to view a representative collection of Venetian painting. Founded in 1807 by Eugène de Beauharnais, Napoleon's viceroy, using the suppressed church and *scuola* of Santa Maria della Carita, it is essentially a sequence of rather gloomy hangars on whose walls many works of exceptional quality are displayed *faute de mieux*. We may hope that one day the municipal powers-that-be will see fit to refurbish the entire suite of rooms, large and small, letting in a little more light and taking down the dingy expanses of hessian against which these pictures are mounted.

Nevertheless here they all are, the Venetian masters of five centuries, the Giorgiones, the Titians, the Tintorettos, the Tiepolos, not perhaps seen to their best advantage, but a quite remarkably rich and wondrous show of one of world art's greatest traditions. The nature of the present book obviously does not allow a detailed survey of the entire collection, but a few of its highlights and incidental joys can certainly be signposted.

You may not wish to linger long in the first room, which concentrates on Venetian Gothic art, but those with memories of Florentine and Sienese painting in the same gold-ground altarpiece form will be tempted to make some telling contrasts. Next comes an imposing sequence of large-scale Renaissance works from the late-fifteenth century, three of them from the church of San Giobbe in the Cannaregio district. 'I, for one, should like to see those three restored to their proper place,' says Hugh Honour in his classic Venetian guide, and we can only agree. In themselves these pictures – a grand yet lyrical throned Madonna with saints by Giovanni Bellini, an idiosyncratic *Presentation of Christ in the Temple* by Vettor Carpaccio, and a fine *Agony in the Garden* by Marco Basaiti (d. 1530), an 'also-ran' of the highest quality – are hugely rewarding, but each cries out for the dimensions and surrounding surface textures which only a church can offer.

The little rooms to the left of this contain some of the most exquisite works in the entire gallery. It is here that you will find those poetically-conceived Madonnas which Bellini painted against vibrantly-detailed landscapes overhung by cloud-mottled skies, just such skies indeed as you can see varying the mountainous backdrop to Venice on a clear spring day. Clouds too establish the mood for Giorgione's seemingly mysterious *La Tempesta*, for which everybody from art historians and philosophers to poets and novelists has tied themselves in knots trying to determine a significance. The soldier, the half-clothed woman, the broken columns and the lightning flash guard their secret (if there is one) complicated still further by the revelation, through X-ray, of overpainted figures in the foreground. All too plain a message, however, is imparted by the likeness of an aged crone, with the words *Col Tempo*, 'With Time', below one of the most striking of Giorgione's images. An equally haunting portrait from a slightly later period (1524) is Lorenzo Lotto's likeness of a young Bergamasc nobleman sitting at his study table, his face turned nervously towards us from his opened book, while a green lizard gazes up at him from a scatter of rose petals.

At the gallery's furthest end two large halls display the classic grand sixteenth-century canvases of Tintoretto and Veronese. The former's scenes from the life of Saint Mark, originally painted for the Scuola Grande di San Marco at San Giovanni e Paolo are unquestionably among his greatest works, distinguished by the sheer insistence of their audacious fantasy. Look, for example, at the extraordinary *Carrying Away of Saint Mark's Body*, in which the painter invests the scene, taking place in what seems to be a kind of city of the dead, with a strange, almost audible sense of fear. As for Veronese's profligate abundance of invention, what better demonstration of it appears than in the massive *Feast in the House of Levi*, a Venetian palace thronged with dogs, halbardiers and lounging onlookers, painted in 1573 for San Giovanni e Paolo's Dominican refectory? Originally this work was entitled *The Last Supper*, but the artist relabelled it after a hair-raising examination by the Inquisition, accusing him of making irreligious mockery of a sacred theme by putting in such a mass of incidental detail.

The profusion of talent from the Venetian eighteenth century is splendidly represented in the subsequent rooms. Landscape painting during this period, in the hands of artists such as Francesco Zuccarelli (1702–1778) and Giuseppe Zaïs (1709–1784), neither of them natives of Venice, took on a distinctly romantic tinge, reflected in that other great Venetian rococo enthusiasm, the fantasy ruin picture, exemplified here by Marco Ricci (1676–1729), nephew of the great Sebastiano, who worked for a time as a scene-painter for the Italian opera in London. Some fascinating small sketches show Tiepolo's genius preparing its ground, and there are several of the graceful, feathery, rather bland pastel portraits for which Rosalba Carriera (1675–1757) made herself an international name.

What we best know in this last-act Venice of masks and mari-onettes are the *vedute*, the prospects of the city and its canals painted by Antonio Canaletto, Francesco Guardi and their satel-lites. Alas, very few of them are actually to be found in Venetian galleries to give you an adequate chance of measuring artistic interpretation with your personal experience of the localities they illustrate, though only an insensitive fool would deny that La Serenissima continues to live up to the marvellous promise of the very different images offered by these two great talents. The solitary Canaletto here, presented by him to the Accademia in 1765, is an enchanting composition of imaginary buildings, while the two Guardis have all the rapt poetic intimacy we associate with this most idiomatic of the *vedutisti*.

The final surprises of the Accademia are provided by Carpaccio and Titian. A special room is given over to the great cycle of scenes from the life of Saint Ursula which Carpaccio painted from 1490 onwards for the now-vanished *scuola* dedicated to the saint, which stood close to the church of San Giovanni e Paolo. Ursula, according to legend, was a Breton princess who married a son of the King of England and was martyred by the Huns, together with her thousand virgin attendants, beneath the walls of the city of Cologne. Carpaccio's treatment of these episodes has all the power of his unique fusion of pageantry with tender-ness and human warmth. It is not always easy to love certain painters, however much you may admire them, but this master has a matchless gift for engaging even the most austere sensibility. The eighteenth-century engraver and writer on art Anton Maria Zanetti (1705–1788) used to hide in the hall of the Scuola di Sant'Orsola just to watch the expressions on the faces of those who saw these romantic pictorial narratives for the first time. We each have our favourites among the nine canvases.

Théophile Gautier, who wrote so ardently of Venice both in poetry and prose, thought the young archer shooting at Saint Ursula in the last picture of all, showing her martyrdom and funeral, was the finest figure, 'of such a proud, youthful, seductive beauty that you might think you were looking at a Cupid by Praxiteles'. I agree, but find the intimacy of the scene showing the saint asleep, dreaming of her devotion to God's service, equally attractive, with the early-morning light sloping through the window, a pair of slippers by the bed, and a little dog crouched on the floor.

As for Titian, whose *Presentation of the Virgin* was painted in 1534–38 to surround the door by which you leave to descend the staircase, why on earth did Ruskin loathe this work so much, calling it 'stupid and uninteresting'? The old woman with her basket of eggs, so essential to the balance of the entire composition but so emphatically Venetian, in a spirit of which Carpaccio himself would have approved, was written off by the Victorian panjandrum as nothing more than painterly ineptitude, 'as dismally ugly and vulgar a filling of a spare corner as was ever daubed on a side scene in a hurry at Drury Lane'. What a luxury it sometimes appears not to have to be always agreeing with Ruskin!

From the Accademia, turn right and retrace your steps to the entrance to Rio Terra Antonio Foscarini, where a left turn takes you as far as the bridge leading over into Campo San Vio. Here until the early nineteenth century stood the church dedicated to Saints Vitus and Modestus, whose feast day saw the successful suppression of Bajamonte Tiepolo's plot against the state in 1310. Every anniversary following, the Doge and Senators came here in solemn procession for a service of thanksgiving. In 1893 the numerous Anglican community in Venice, both British and American, was allowed its own place of worship on the site, and though '*la chiesa inglese*', dedicated of course to Saint George, is not quite the flourishing affair it was in the days of Mrs Bronson, Lady Layard and other expatriate *grandes dames*, there is still a real pleasure in the sheer incongruity of mattins, holy communion and Victorian hymn tunes with the sound of *vaporetto* hooters and the slap of Grand Canal backwash outside the decorous stained-glass windows as an accompaniment.

Beyond the *campo*, in the narrow neck of the Dorsoduro, is the quarter's smartest residential zone, an area of hugely desirable tranquillity in the very heart of noisy central Venice. Not for nothing was this the spot where Peggy Guggenheim, patroness and art collector, chose to settle, together with the works she had gathered over several decades spent pursuing a discerning enthusiasm for twentieth-century European and American art. Was her residence here altogether accidental? A certain Michelangelo Guggenheim, to whom she was doubtless connected, figures among the earliest benefactors of the Correr Museum.

In that museum itself is the model for the Palazzo Venier dei Leoni, where Peggy Guggenheim came to live. Begun in 1749 to a design by Lorenzo Boschetti (dates unknown), the building was, for whatever reason, unfinished, but the single surviving storey gives the passing voyager along the Grand Canal some notion of what splendour the Venier, who could boast two doges in the family, were able to command. The noble house had several branches, and this one was known as 'dei Leoni' because they apparently kept lions in the garden here.

The only lions you will find here now are those of the great modern traditions of painting and sculpture. Cubism is memorably represented by Braque's *The Clarinet* and the figure of a poet by Picasso, and the wonderful bust of Russian modernism on the eve of the 1917 revolution strikes powerful notes in the work of Kandinsky and Malevich. There are Italian futurists, Balla and Boccioni, from the same crucial period, an exceptional equestrian bronze by Marino Marini, as well as Surrealist works by Salvador Dali and Peggy Guggenheim's former husband Max Ernst. Her native America is shown to advantage in paintings by Mark Rothko, Jackson Pollock and the Armenian abstract expressionist Arshile Gorki. Taken altogether, this is unquestionably the most significant collection of its kind in the whole of Italy, a bracing corrective to aesthetic appetites overdosed on the historic traditions of vernacular art.

A former denizen of Palazzo Venier dei Leoni – which you reach by a walk from San Vio along a *fondamenta* and over a bridge into a tree-shaded *campiello* – was the Marchesa Casati, wife of a rich industrialist, who made a name for herself at the beginning of this century, both as a flamboyant party-giver and as the incarnation of that kind of melodramatic beauty which society portrait painters of the period, such as Giovanni Boldini and Jacques-Emile Blanche, loved to capture. She was studied, perhaps not without a touch of envy, by the young Lady Diana Manners (later Diana Cooper) who watched her walking her pet leopard in Piazza San Marco. Many years later, by now a celebrated social leader in her own right, she discovered the Marchesa residing in London, a raddled shadow of her former self, living on the dubious comforts provided by pills and syringes.

Hints of decadence have always enhanced the fascination of Venice, and the Ca'Dario, next door to the Guggenheim, is wreathed in gilded notoriety. The palace's entertainingly fussy façade is probably the work of one of the Lombardo family, created around 1480 for a diplomat named Giovanni Dario. During the first half of the nineteenth century it was the residence of Rawdon Brown, a friend of Ruskin and one of those tireless English researchers into Venetian history who have done so much, over the past two hundred years, to shape the city's identity as a cultural icon. The Ca'Dario is always said to bring bad luck to its owners: Brown committed suicide, and a later tenant, Kit Lambert, manager of The Who pop group came to a sad end, as did the palace's most recent master, who killed himself after a financial scandal.

The narrow *calle* at the back of the palace leads to a bridge with a delightful view along a canal with a *fondamenta* on each side, stretching down to the Zattere and the Canale della Giudecca. Beyond this, a left turn will take you, should you need it, to a *traghetto* (gondola ferry) crossing to Santa Maria del Giglio on the opposite bank of the Grand Canal. If you walk straight ahead, however, you come to the fifteenth-century Gothic church of San Gregorio, now used as a workshop for art restoration,

162

and passing under the *sottoportego*, you emerge at last beside one of the most familiar and best-loved of Venetian landmarks, without which the city's profile is now quite unimaginable.

It is indeed hard to conceive of the Basilica of Santa Maria della Salute as not having always been here, dominating one flank of the entrance to the Grand Canal. The stupendous assertions made by this great white marble drum, crowned by a high dome and

adorned with balletic statuary, have only been sounding for three hundred and fifty years, not a very long time in the history of Venice. The architect was Baldassare Longhena and the occasion of its founding in 1631 was a thanksgiving by the senate and populace for liberation from the last terrible visitation of plague on the city during the previous year, during which a staggering thirty percent of the inhabitants had died.

The basilica, intended to underline the Serene Republic's special relationship with the Virgin Mary, also provided its artistic creator with a brilliant opportunity for displaying his professional prowess and conceptual originality. Longhena declared that he wanted it to be 'strange, worthy and beautiful . . . in the shape of a round machine, such as had never been seen or invented, either whole or in part, in any other church in the city'. The government, in the manner of several governments in other countries since, approved the scheme as long as it made a good impression without costing too much, but, although the million wooden foundation piles were laid almost at once, the building was not finished until five years later after Longhena's death in 1682.

Why is the Salute such a triumphant success? Why does the merest recollection of it fire the heart with longing to return to Venice, a hankering after all things Venetian? Perhaps this has something to do with its mystical shape, that of a crown for the Madonna, whose statue, under a starry circlet, tops the cupola. Maybe it derives from the handsomeness of its exterior, decked out with huge marble volutes, buttresses, doors between tall columns and deeply incised arches. Surely it owes much to the sublime skill of Longhena's interior plan, which 'concentrates the mind wonderfully' by creating vistas within vistas through the use of an octagonal double arcade framing six small chapels, but focusing on an oblong chancel dominated by a magnificent high altar, surmounted by a miraculous Greek icon brought here from Crete in 1672 by the great military campaigner and future doge Francesco Morosini. Those who write off the Baroque as all frills and nonsense will find it necessary to revise their opinions when confronted by the church's relative plainness – white stucco, grey marble, with only a cunningly-patterned floor to set off this simplicity.

The sacristy, reached through a door to the left of the choir, contains paintings and furnishings from the demolished church of Santo Spirito in Isola, whose ceiling, by the Tuscan Giuseppe Salviati, you will have seen above the apse, and whose bronze candelabra adorn the high altar. Finest among the sacristy's treasures is a colourful early Titian, painted in 1511 and strongly influenced by Giorgione, showing Saint Mark enthroned above Saint Roch, an athletic, curly-maned Saint Sebastian, and the two doctor saints Cosmas and Damian, dressed in the Venetian robes appropriate to their calling. There is also a powerfully-conceived *Wedding Feast at Cana*, signed and dated 1551, by Tintoretto, which Ruskin enthusiastically terms 'perhaps the most perfect example which human art has produced of the utmost possible force and sharpness of shadow united with richnes of local colour'.

From below the steps going down from the church to canal level, lavish marble flights aptly compared by Henry James to the train of a dress, you can turn to admire Santa Maria della Salute and share in the almost universal feeling that few buildings in Venice create so satisfying and appropriate an effect of swagger and majesty, combined with sheer beauty of line. 'Is it possible,' asked yet another illustrious Victorian Venetophile, Robert Browning, 'that wise men disapprove of those quaint buttresses?' Maybe, but for the rest of us this building is Omega to the Alpha of Saint Mark's in Venice's visual alphabet.

Now walk along the quay, round to the very point of the Dorsoduro, the Punta della Dogana. The fine porticoed custom-house building behind you, with its two bronze atlanti bearing a golden ball topped by the figure of Fortune, is the work of the Triestine architect Giuseppe Benoni (1618–1684). 'Dogana' derives from an Arabic word meaning an official post for declaring trade goods, and from this Venetian form comes the French word *douâne* meaning a customs office.

Together with the Salute, this was a favourite subject for view-painters: Canaletto included it in several *vedute* and Turner, in the early nineteenth century, made it the theme of some evocative watercolours. Standing here on a sunny morning, looking out across the blue water between Saint Mark's, San Giorgio Maggiore and the Giudecca, you can hardly fail to sense that exhilaration with which Venice at its most visually generous kindles the senses into renewed life. You have made the acquaintance of the city itself. Now, across those waves, the islands tempt you to embark, islands where the first idea of a sea-girt republic, free and serene, was born.

7 : To the Islands

Those visiting Venice for the first time nearly always leave the
islands of the lagoon until the end of their stay, and this order of
priorities is perfectly understandable. Yet from the purely historical and geographical aspects, such places ought to form a beginning to any experience of Venice, since the origins and progress
of the city and its people are absolutely inconceivable without
this particular visual context, that of the small, half-rural island
community. In such spots as Torcello and Burano you are closer

than you will ever be in Saint Mark's Square or on the Rialto Bridge to the antique, half-legendary world of those early settlers on the mudbanks in the days of Huns and Goths, of Tribuni Maritimi and Doges with names like Paoluccio Anafesto, Obelerio de'Antenori and Giustiniano Partecipazio.

Before you absolutely quit the city for the open waters of the lagoon, however, there are two islands to be visited which essentially form part of metropolitan Venice itself, and whose position, to the south of the Dorsoduro, lends the ultimate definition to the classic Venetian townscape of palaces and churches rising sheer from the blue waves crowded with shipping.

The first of these faces you as you stand on the Fondamenta delle Zattere, with the cranes and oil rigs of Porto Marghera distantly visible through the haze to your right. This is the long, narrow island of La Giudecca, formerly known as Spina Longa (literally 'long spine' because of its resemblance to a fishbone) but given its present name in the early Middle Ages, either because the first Venetian Jewish community lived here, or because it was used as a place of exile for nobility both fractious and factious, who were declared '*giudicati*', 'judged'. Other more fortunate patricians liked it for the sea breezes and the gardens where it was customary for everyone to go and pick mulberries on the Monday following the Festa del Redentore, the Feast of the Redeemer, which falls on the third Sunday in July.

Alas, there are not many gardens left on the Giudecca, and until recently the smarter Venetians gave it a wide berth, but owing possibly to the astronomical cost of decent-sized apartments in the centre of the city, the island has lately become a fashionable retreat from the tourist-choked banks of the Grand Canal, and is much favoured by wealthy artists, retired expatriates and all the sort of people you might reasonably expect to find living on the elegant *piani nobili* of palaces by the Accademia Bridge or in chic apartments near Santa Maria della Salute. The place nevertheless manages to retain much of that air of '*una zona popolare*', 'an area for ordinary folk', which attracts these affluent incomers in the first place, and there is much pleasure to be had from walking among its quiet, unpretending alleys and courts, or along its broad *fondamente*.

Crossing from the Zattere, you land on what used to be the separate island of San Biagio, with the Disneyland castle of the Stucky flour mill towering to your right and the church of Santa Eufemia immediately in front of you. Though rarely open, this is worth a glance if the doors are open. The early mediaeval building was extensively overhauled in the eighteenth century, with stucco decoration on the ceiling, a whole set of handsome if slightly frigid altarpieces and frescoes by such minor but accomplished artists as Giambattista Canal (1745–1825) and Francesco Cappella (1714–1784) and a fine *Virgin and Child* in marble by Giovanni Maria Morlaiter. From among the surviving furnishings from former ages, a triptych – or part of it – by Bartolomeo Vivarini stands out.

It is hard nowadays to visualize San Biagio as the romantic spot it undoubtedly once was, a place of little orchards and gardens surrounding a convent, a home for penitent prostitutes and a pilgrim's hostel. Alfred de Musset celebrates it in some artless little verses he wrote after a good lunch at one of its *trattorie*, about going to gather verbena in the flowery meadows of '*Saint-Blaise, à la Zuecca*' and longing to die there. Most of its charm has vanished, and epicures nowadays would probably rather walk on along the *fondamenta* to Harry's Dolci, a superior sort of ice-cream parlour owned by the management of Harry's Bar. Crossing the Ponte Lungo beyond, with its view down the broad *rio*, you arrive at last before the chaste marble façade of the church of the Redentore.

Like the Salute this was built in fulfilment of a vow, following a severe plague epidemic which struck Venice in 1576. The architect was Andrea Palladio, who completed it in 1592 and whose design, deriving its impact from a very carefully reined-in simplicity, is one of his most effective. The façade is a sober variant on classical themes – pilasters of mingled orders above a broad flight of steps and topped by a sharply-angled pediment – and the interior leads us up a vaulted nave towards the high altar, backed by Corinthian columns and surmounted by a tabernacle designed by the Bolognese artist Giuseppe Mazza (1652–1740). You will want to pause in front of pictures like Alvise Vivarini's spirited *Madonna and Child with Musical Angels* in the sacristy, the late, unfinished *Baptism of Christ* by Veronese in the second chapel on the right, and an *Ecstasy of Saint Francis* from the talented and affecting brush of Carlo Saraceni (1580–1620), a Venetian who went to Rome and worked with Caravaggio, but came home to die in his native city. Yet it is the Palladian context, white Istrian marble against pale stucco, the overarching high windows incised into the vaulting, an informed classicism mingling erudition and wit, that ultimately enraptures the onlooker or inspires the worshipper.

The Redentore is associated with the most romantic of Venetian festivals, one which commemorates the annual visit of the Doge and senators to the church on the third Sunday in July. Nowadays at this time, though the ducal pomps of the Republic exist no longer, the traditional bridge of boats is still thrown over the water from the Zattere, crossed by thousands on the vigil night of the feast itself for the purpose of praying and lighting candles in the church, while the skies are ablaze with stupendous fireworks and Venice, somewhat unusually, stays up all night long to welcome the dawn with picnics and bathing at the Lido.

Mary McCarthy, in her fine sequence of impressions *Venice Observed*, evokes the occasion's full vibrancy, the palaces rocking with explosions, the brilliant colours reflected in the canals, the pictorial echoes of Guardi, Bassano and Carpaccio, and the second firework display which takes place at San Giorgio Maggiore. After this, she says, 'you are supposed to be rowed to the Lido to see the sunrise. As a gondolier explained to me gravely, the true colours of nature refresh the eye after the fires of artifice. There spoke Venice, the eternal connoisseur, in the voice of her eternal gondolier.'

Well, perhaps. It is indeed to San Giorgio that you can now cross from the Giudecca, taking the *vaporetto* outside the church of Le Zitelle, further along the *fondamenta*, designed around 1580 by an architect named Jacopo Bozzetto, using a Palladian model. Since Bozzetto's dates are unknown and his name in Italian means 'sketch' or 'outline', one is tempted to wonder whether he actually existed. The Zitelle is officially styled Santa Maria della Presentazione, but got its nickname from the refuge for poor spinsters – *zitelle* – attached to it, famous for a much-admired pattern of lacemaking known as *punto in aria*.

The tiny island of San Giorgio Maggiore, off the Giudecca's eastern tip, was originally covered with gardens and boasted a mill established by Doge Angelo Partecipazio (811–827) for grinding corn for his palace. It was his successor Tribuno Memmo who in 982 gave it to the Morosini family as a compensation for wrong done to them. The Benedictine monastery they founded here soon became one of the most prosperous religious houses in all Venice, receiving, besides the body of Doge Sebastiano Ziani in 1178, the relics of Saint Stephen the Protomartyr himself, brought from Constantinople by the doughty crusader Ordelafo Falier (he apparently carried the saint's coffin personally in his arms to the high altar of San Giorgio). On Christmas night, the vigil of Saint Stephen's feast, the Doge and Senators would make another of their seemingly endless round of devout expeditions, to worship at the shrine.

Quite why the monastery and its island took Saint George as their dedicatee is unknown. From mediaeval times until the present day the place has preserved its character as a garden retreat, sheltering memories of the days when the Morosini, who kept a house here, entertained their guests with philosophic debates, and the exiled Cosimo de'Medici of Florence sought refuge among the monks in 1433. Like the rest of his family Cosimo was an instinctive patron of the arts, and during his short stay he commissioned his own architect Michelozzo Michelozzi to build a library to house the monks' collection of books and manuscripts, together with his own gift of incunabula.

It may seem a pity that this building had to be dismantled when, during the late sixteenth century, the Benedictines, by now very rich, began a wholesale reconstruction, choosing Andrea Palladio as their principal architect, but his total achievement at San Giorgio is so monumental that we can hardly regret the loss of one treasure too much when another such as this takes its place. Palladio was not a native Venetian – he was born Andrea di Piero at Vicenza on the *terraferma* – but he had an extraordinary sensitivity to Venice's uniqueness, which is why his church and conventual buildings here create such an indelible image. A profoundly cultivated artist, whose reinterpretation of the principles of the Roman architectural theorist Vitruvius was imbued with a deep feeling for the spirit of antiquity, he took his nickname from Pallas Athene, goddess of wisdom, and very appropriate this was.

The church of San Giorgio was begun in 1566 and work was still in progress when Palladio died in 1580, the entire building being completed thirty years later. In spirit, however, the creation is essentially his own throughout, formulating its own pure idiom of space, depth and decorative coherence, untroubled by any sense of needless striving for those effects of which the architect is always so sublimely confident. From the façade's authoritative grandeur to the cool beauty of the interior, with its avenue of columns leading with such magnificent inevitability to the grandly conceived chancel, this is one of the most richly satisfying buildings in all Venice.

Its riches extend to some excellent painting and sculpture. On either side of the door as you enter, acting as pendants to the monument to the enlightened Doge Leonardo Donà (1606–1612) are figures of the Four Evangelists, vivid stucco modelling by Alessandro Vittoria. Above the first altar on the right is an *Adoration of the Shepherds*, painted around 1592 and probably the last major work of Jacopo Bassano, who brings to it his usual hankering after country life and a world where animals matter as much to God as do their human masters. Immediately to the right of the high altar is a brisk *Virgin with Saints* by Sebastiano Ricci, dated 1708 and making a deliberate appeal to our sense of painterly continuity in the Venetian tradition of Tintoretto and Veronese.

The former dominates the upper end of the church. Above the grandiose altar designed by the Greek artist Antonio Vassilacchi, with a set of early Baroque choir stalls beyond it adorned by reliefs showing scenes from Saint Benedict's life, hang two of Tintoretto's most ambitious projects, a *Last Supper* and a *Fall of Manna*, probably painted in 1564 but installed here three decades afterwards when the church itself was nearing completion. Each perfectly demonstrates that instinct which the painter shared with his contemporary and rival Veronese, for a spirituality grounded in the everyday world. Notice, at the edge of the *Last Supper*, beyond all the angels and radiance, the servant girl who enters the room with plates of food. She is merely doing her appointed task, yet she too is momentarily transfigured by the occasion's divine singularity, a wonderful illustration by the devout Tintoretto of God's universal presence.

In the corridor to the right of the high altar lies one of the monastery's earliest benefactors, the great Doge Domenico Michiel (1118–1130). It was he who pledged Venetian assistance during the First Crusade, who installed the two granite columns in the Piazzetta and who brought Saint Isidore's body to its chapel in the basilica of Saint Mark. After such a vigorous career, he preferred, not surprisingly, to spend his last years as a monk in the convent of San Giorgio. On his tomb (not contemporary, but created in 1636 by Baldassare Longhena) is a Latin epitaph reading 'The terror of the Greeks lies here'.

Above this corridor, in an upper chapel, a conclave of Catholic cardinals gathered in 1800 to elect a successor to the hapless Pope Pius VI who had died the previous year as a prisoner of Napoleon. It was centuries since a pope had been named anywhere else but in Rome, but the city was now in French hands, so the princes of the church found it safer to meet here in Venice, which had recently passed to Austrian control through the Treaty of Campoformio. Among their number was Henry Benedict Stuart, grandson of the exiled King James II of Great Britain, and, since the death of his drunken, feckless brother Charles Edward, 'Bonnie Prince Charlie', the last direct Jacobite claimant to the British throne. Though he did not seriously expect to be nominated (the choice ultimately fell on Gregorio Barnaba Chiaromonti as Pope Pius VII), 'Cardinal York', as he was known, did find some joy on this rather fraught occasion, since the actual King of England, George III, sent a message to announce that he was to be paid a yearly pension. Those with Jacobite sympathies have always taken this to mean that George himself felt guilty as the descendant of a Hanoverian 'usurper', but it seems more likely that the monarch, enjoying a brief moment of sanity, was motivated by a mixture of compassion and national honour. The Stuart cardinal was a lazy spendthrift with a dubious private life, but as a royal Briton he must not be allowed to starve.

From the church you can either climb the campanile for an awesome panorama across the city and the waters of the lagoon, or visit the convent next door. This is now partly given over to the Fondazione Giorgio Cini, founded by the industrialist Count Vittorio Cini in memory of his son, as an institute for the study of Venetian culture. It is not normally open to the general public, but every summer a sequence of art historical lectures and conferences, musical recitals and splendidly mounted exhibitions give you the opportunity of seeing some of the grander monastic rooms.

Among these are Palladio's monumental refectory, begun in 1560, his cloister of nineteen years later, and its forerunner, built by Giovanni Antonio di Buora (d. 1513) around 1510. Up the opulent sweep of Longhena's grand staircase is a gorgeous library by the same architect, now a rich resource for scholars of every aspect of Venice's historical and artistic legacy. And, superb as all these things are, their beauty is enhanced by San Giorgio's setting. There is nothing quite like that vista towards the Salute and Saint Mark's from the wave-slapped Istrian marble steps outside. No wonder one Venetian poet exclaimed, 'Surely it looks as if done with a paintbrush', while Henry James extolled that 'suffusion of rosiness' in which the little island always seems to be bathed.

From the other side of San Giorgio Maggiore you look across to the long, narrow line of the Lido. The name, derived from the Latin *litus*, 'shore', has got rather oddly and incorrectly applied to all sorts of other places throughout Europe, including a famous Parisian nightclub and any number of municipal swimming baths, but this is the actual and original Lido, where some of the oldest of the settlements took root which eventually became the independent republic of Venice. Nowadays little remains of these ancient ports and townships, and the slender spit of land is given over to seaside hotels, shops, restaurants and quiet residential avenues. Most visitors are content to head straight for the main beaches at the foot of the avenue leading down from the *vaporetto* landing stages, but the more adventurous may prefer to take a bus to Alberoni at the island's southern end, deliciously quiet amid sand dunes and pine woods, from which now and then bulky cargo ships can be glimpsed easing their way down the channel dividing the Lido from the neighbouring Pellestrina, essentially a continuation of the same fragment of ancient shore-line.

Historical traces here are comparatively few. Of Malamocco, once the seat of Venetian government before its move to the Rialto, nothing whatever survives its twelfth-century destruction by an earthquake. The village of that name, towards the Alberoni, has a few traces of mediaeval buildings and a very imposing campanile adjoining the church of Santa Maria dell'Assunzione, but you would hardly know that here, from 720 to 810, the early Doges consolidated their power. Travellers with literary interests will want to visit the Grand Hotel des Bains for its associations with Thomas Mann's novella *Der Tod in Venedig (Death in Venice)* and the decidedly operatic film treatment of the story made by Luchino Visconti, not to speak of its more refined handling in a genuine opera by Benjamin Britten. They may also recall the Lido as the setting for one of Shelley's finest poems, *Julian and Maddalo*, which re-enacts his rides along the beach in the company of Byron, whose sensual enjoyment of all things Venetian seems to have shocked the idealistic young poet. In those days the place was congenially empty, and invested with the kind of forlornness calculated to appeal to a romantic sensibility. Shelley talks of:

> the bank of sand which breaks the flow
> Of Adria towards Venice: a bare strand
> Of hillocks heaped from ever-shifting sand . . .
> . . . an uninhabited seaside
> Which the lone fisher, when his nets are dried,
> Abandons, and no other object breaks
> The waste . . .

Scattered between the Lido and Venice itself, you will notice several small islands, all of which were used, until the fall of the Serene Republic, as residences for religious orders engaged in various sorts of beneficent enterprise. San Clemente, for example, was a resting place for voyagers returning from Jerusalem, San Servolo was and still is the home of a mental asylum, formerly administered by the friars known as Fatebene Fratelli (literally, 'do well, brothers') as a hospital for lunatic patricians, while on La Grazia a community of Capuchin nuns looked after the welfare of pilgrims going to and from various Italian shrines further south.

Most interesting to us now is the island of San Lazzaro, which you can visit from the Lido itself. In 1717 the Senate decreed the removal of a leper hospital here to the neighbourhood of San Giovanni e Paolo, and with a typically Venetian mixture of xenophilia and opportunism gave the site to a community of fugitive Armenians, formerly established in the Peloponnese, under the leadership of a monk named Manug Mechitar ('consoler') who had established a Benedictine monastery in the Greek port of Methoni. Using their own Armenian Orthodox church ceremonies, the monks, known as the Mechitarist Fathers, not only set up their monastic house here, but founded a printing press for books in their own language and a boys' school. Over the past three centuries the monks, in addition to their priceless collection of early Armenian manuscripts, have gathered together an amazing cabinet of curiosities, including Egyptian mummies, Indian paintings, some good Venetian pictures by such masters as Bassano, Guardi, Canaletto and Ricci, and relics of Byron, who turned to the study of Armenian as a relief from boredom during his stay in the city in 1816. The details the monks gave him of their people's history, one of endless bitterness and oppression, appealed to his instinctive championship of the world's underdogs, but the Armenian language presented him with some tough challenges. 'I found that my mind wanted something craggy to break upon; and this, as the most difficult thing I could discover here for an amusement, I have chosen, to torture me into attention.' He got on very well with the fathers, praising their gentleness, learning and devotion, and even went so far as to plan an Armenian–English dictionary and grammar.

So much for the lagoon's southern stretch. To reach the more northerly islands, you need to walk from Saint Mark's towards the Fondamenta Nuove, the stretch of waterfront beyond San Giovanni e Paolo and the Gesuiti. Here you look out across a vista very different from the busy waters on the other side of the city. An almost magnetic sense of tranquillity prevails in the Guardi-like prospect of distant islands framed between the blue absolutes of sea and sky.

Théophile Gautier, during the early nineteenth century, wrote some beautiful poems based on what seem to have been specifically Venetian memories. Several of these were transformed by Hector Berlioz into his glorious song cycle *Les Nuits d'été*, written in 1830. I always think of these pieces when starting out on this particular island excursion across the northern lagoon, sometimes recalling the quiet melancholy of the lover in *Sur les lagunes* who laments 'Alas, that is my bitter fate, to go over the seas without love!' and sometimes remembering the exhilaration of the young girl in *L'Ile inconnue* who cries, 'Take me to the faithful shore where love endures for ever!' The journey may easily respond to both these moods.

Along the Fondamenta Nuove the flower stalls sell chrysanthemums, the archetypal cemetery flower of Italy which is considered bad luck or at any rate bad form to produce on any other occasion than a funeral or a visit to the grave. No Venetian expedition is complete without a voyage to the island of the dead, little San Michele, embowered in its cypress trees behind high walls, enclosing what many consider to be not merely the loveliest of Italian graveyards, but the most impressive spot in the whole world as regards the choice of a final resting place.

The church of San Michele itself, which greets you as you land from the *vaporetto*, is one of the most important Venetian Renaissance buildings, the first major statement, indeed, of the style which the architect Mauro Coducci imprinted so memorably elsewhere on the features of the city during the late fifteenth century. Commissioned by the friars of the Camaldolese order (named after its earliest home at Camaldoli in the Tuscan mountains), the church was begun in 1469 and completed in 1530 by the addition of the little hexagonal chapel to the left, known as the Cappella Emiliana, designed by Guglielmo Grigi, who died in the same year. He is always called 'Bergamasco', from his native city of Bergamo, where the Cappella Colleoni, attached to the basilica of Santa Maria Maggiore, perhaps offered the inspiration for this adornment to an already outstanding work.

Calm understatement is the keynote of Coducci's façade, crowned by its characteristic curved pediment and discoursing an architectural language learned in part from the classic Tempio Malatestiano at Rimini by Leon Battista Alberti. Within, we can see how the architect was still in the process of learning, for there is a general impression of the church's various sections not quite fitting together, despite eye-catching detail among the various furnishings, such as the handsome Renaissance arch to the Cappella della Croce and the sacristy ceiling, whose perspectives are by Romualdo Mauro (1720–1768), member of a distinguished family of operatic scene painters. The Cappella Emiliana itself was paid for by a rich widow named Margherita Vitturi, and still contains its original decorative scheme of small altars featuring marble relief sculpture by the Lombard artist Giovanni Antonio de Carona (1477–1534).

Beyond the church and its cloister stretches the cemetery, dating only from the Napoleonic period but now an integral part of the Venetian experience. Apart from certain wealthy families who were able to buy plots and maintain vaults here, the average citizen of Venice may only stay buried on San Michele for twenty years before being carted off to a boneyard elsewhere on the lagoon. Exceptions to the rule, however, are certain distinguished foreigners, such as the composer Igor Stravinsky, his celebrated Ballets Russes impresario Sergei Diaghilev, and the poet Ezra Pound, as well as poor Frederick Rolfe, Baron Corvo, for whom burial here was a sort of accolade for his profound apprehensions of Venetian life. A quiet stroll among the cypress alleys and the neat, sometimes rather bunker-like tombs (James Morris, in his book on Venice, calls them 'awful monuments', but some are great fun and a few are genuinely dignified and attractive) makes a pleasing prelude to a morning among the islands.

From San Michele it is but a short crossing to Murano, whence derive all those glass gondolas taken halfway across the world by tourists who may not have ventured further than the shops in Saint Mark's Square. This island of glass played a historic role in the development of the Venetian economy. The craft of glass-blowing established here was probably a survival from Roman times, but must have received real impetus from Venice's contacts with Byzantium and the Muslim East. Its mystery was guarded with elaborate precautions: no glassworker was allowed to leave Venetian territory, and some were not even permitted to quit Murano itself. In compensation, the *muranesi* were given their own laws and administrative council, maintained their own Golden Book of local aristocracy (which held parity in marriage with the patricians of the city), minted ceremonial coinage and enjoyed immunity from the Serenissima's legal officials.

The great age of Venetian glass arrived with the technology for producing 'crystal' in the early sixteenth century, and it is the goblets, dishes and chandeliers of this and subsequent periods which form the centrepiece of the Museo dell'Arte Vetraria, a huge display of 4,000 pieces arranged in two palaces beside the island's main canal. After the bottom dropped out of the market in the late seventeenth century, when French and German glass-blowers purloined and adapted the trade secrets, the industry might easily have become extinct here, but a surprising recovery followed the Republic's fall, and now much is produced that is beautiful and innovative, as opposed to the trippers' knick-knacks which form its staple. Nowadays there is no longer any secrecy involved in glass-blowing techniques, and you have plenty of chances, while on Murano, to watch the miraculous process of creation, but you can still understand why it was always believed that something special and indefinable in the island's atmosphere made its furnaces unique. As the Jacobean traveller James Howell wrote: 'Some impute it to the quality of the circumambient air that hangs over the place, which is purified and attenuated by the concurrence of so many fires as are in those furnaces night and day perpetually, for they are like the vestal fire, which never goes out. And it is well known that some airs make more qualifying impressions than others.'

There is more to Murano than showrooms for glassware. In its role as a microcosm of Venice itself, the island possesses several interesting churches along the banks of its main canals, and one of these stands close beside the museum. This is the large basilica of SS. Maria e Donato, an impressive piece of twelfth-century Veneto-Byzantine work, restored with rather a heavy hand between 1858 and 1873. The restorers, in their misguided piety, tried to return the church to its original brick construction, but the result, especially from the outside, seems unnecessarily garish and forbidding.

Inside, nevertheless, you receive a pleasant imitation of the building as a religious palimpsest over which generations have scribbled their devotion. Witness the slender praying Virgin in the gold-ground mosaic of the main apse, and similar early mediaeval mosaic work in the floor patterns, perhaps designed by artists working during the same period on the pavement of Saint Mark's itself. The date 1140, in abbreviated Latin wording, is fixed in the central roundel. Witness also the most engaging little early Venetian altarpieces in the left aisle, especially one showing San Donato between two donors, members of the Memmo family, painted in 1310, and, for contrast, a stylish brace of Baroque saints on the high altar. These are two local patrons, Lorenzo Giustiniani and that unfortunate Theodore who had to make room for the most prestigious Evangelist. As for Donatus himself, carried off from the Ionian island of Cephalonia, which later became a Venetian colony (and still later part of the British Empire), his relics are preserved here, together with those of a dragon he is said to have slain by spitting at it.

Walking back past the museum and following the curve of the canal, you cross the Ponte Vivarini, the work of the sixteenth-century architect Francesco Marcolini, with the tall Palazzo da Mula on your left. This was originally a mediaeval palace, built in days when Murano was used as a country retreat by Venetian families. Though in part redesigned during the Renaissance, it keeps its Gothic windows and little Byzantine decorative reliefs, as well as the remains of a garden.

Nearby is the church of San Pietro Martire, founded in 1348 as part of a Dominican monastery, but raised in its present form in 1474 after a fire. Most visitors come here now to see two exceptional works by Giovanni Bellini. The first is a truly lyrical *Virgin and Saints* from the year 1488, in which the central drama of Augustine and Mark presenting Doge Agostino Barbaro to the throned Madonna and Child is set against a rich purple curtain, a great sweep of Veneto landscape with distant mountains, a trio of birds, peacock, partridge and crane, clustered around a marble balustrade. The second, a lively *Assumption of the Virgin*, painted during the artist's final phase in the early 1500s, has a yet lovelier background prospect, with little towers set on wooded hills, up which riders urge their horses, while a shepherd takes a nap under a tree.

From this realm of glass and glass-blowers, the boat takes you north-eastwards through the tranquil channels of the lagoon, past a scatter of small islands, to a place which for me remains one of the most appealing in the world. A trip to Burano is always oddly like a journey into the country, accentuated by the presence of the little green islet of Mazzorbo tacked onto one side of it, covered in orchards and garden plots. The houses here are rows of low-pitched canalside cottages, humble enough if contrasted with Venetian *palazzi* or even with their equivalents on Murano, but rendered genuinely attractive by their varied colour-washes of pink, ochre, russet, blue or green. Burano began as a fishing community, and the presence of boats, nets and tackle along the island's canals is still more than merely decorative. Its significance in the economy of the Republic became paramount during the sixteenth and seventeenth centuries, when its most important cottage industry, the making of lace for ruffs, collars, handkerchiefs and sleeves, became a major Venetian monopoly.

Made on the traditional pillow known as a *tombolo*, the Burano

laces, worked by women seated on special low-pitched chairs at their cottage doors, achieved an amazing delicacy in pattern and execution, several designs, such as the famous *punto in aria* and *punto a rosette*, fetching the highest prices throughout Europe. From Spain, where King Philip II's haughty grandees adorned their black satin doublets with the filigree artifice of some humble girl on a distant Adriatic lagoon, to England, where Queen Elizabeth and her ladies sported massive starched ruffs of 'Venice point', the skill of the *buranelle* seemed a guarantee of enduring prosperity.

Alas, even the best-kept secrets have their price, and for all the state could do in the way of safeguards and penalties, certain islanders were eventually lured away with generous inducements from Colbert, Louis XIV's shrewd, patriotic minister. Determined to make French industries as competitive and self-sufficient as possible and to undercut Venetian prices, he had the lacemakers of France taught the essential Italian skills of the art, and the predictable result was yet another blow at the ailing Serenissima's economic substructure. The lacemaking on Burano was nevertheless revived in the early years of the present century, and now you can watch the various stages of the process carried out by deft fingers moving to and fro across the *tombolo*.

Burano is a small, compact community, and a walk along its canal banks, from whatever direction, will bring you at last to the *campo* in front of the pleasantly sprawling sixteenth-century church of San Martino. The building contains several worthwhile canvases, an *Adoration of the Shepherds* by Francesco Fontebasso, with whose late-Rococo style you will be more familiar in the form of ceiling frescoes in Venetian churches, an important early Tiepolo *Crucifixion* and *Saint Mark with Saints*, an especially fine example of the work of Bellini's talented assistant Gerolamo da Santacroce, who painted it in 1541.

The church also contains a memorial to Burano's most famous son, the long-lived composer Baldassare Galuppi (1703–1785), known indeed as Il Buranello. Galuppi was a hugely versatile talent, at his ease whether writing oratorios, cantatas or keyboard music, who did more than anyone else during the mid-eighteenth century to lay the foundations of the comic opera style embodied at its most perfect in the stage works of Wolfgang Amadeus Mozart. His career took him out of Italy, first of all to London and then to Saint Petersburg, where Catherine the Great employed him to bring an Italianate polish to musical performances at the Winter Palace, Peterhof and Tsarskoe Selo. After several years in Russia, the footloose maestro felt homesick for his native lagoon and came back at last to Venice, where he took over the important post of musical director at the orphanage of the Incurabili. After his work passed out of fashion in the succeeding century, he was known only from the title of Browning's poem 'A Toccata of Galuppi's', which uses the associations of his music to evoke the vanished hedonism of the Serene Republic in the years before its fall, but the revival of interest in Italian 'pre-classical' music has revealed him to listeners once more as a composer of real resourcefulness and charm.

From Burano it is possible, if you have time, to make the journey by boat to the island of San Francesco nel Deserto, the refuge of the Franciscans in the lagoon since the saint himself was said to have landed here in 1220 during a storm on his return voyage from the East, where he had unsuccessfully tried to convert the Egyptian Mamelukes to Christianity. Having calmed the winds and waves, he and his followers set about building a retreat, encouraged by the chirping of the birds. Francis carried with him a pine staff, which burst into miraculous shoots when he stuck it in the ground. An Italian guidebook in my possession, dating from the early years of the present century and translated into enjoyably faulty English, tells me that the staff 'at once grew radishes' – which would have been an additional miracle, had the author not simply meant 'roots', 'radici'. The tree survives, as does the Franciscan monastery with its little church and double cloister.

Those in more of a hurry, however, will want to pass straight on towards the ultimate goal of most travellers on this particular voyage, the island of Torcello, divided from Burano by a narrow channel. Nowadays the walk up from the landing stage along a canal flanked by tall reed beds, the ineffable quiet and solitude of this place and the care obviously taken by those responsible for it not to violate this tranquillity with too many of what the Italians call 'touristic installations' would hardly lead you to believe that it was formerly one of the busiest, most powerful islands in the northern Adriatic, a city of palaces, with an independent government, an episcopal see more venerable than that of Venice itself, and its own charters, rights and privileges.

Torcello was first settled by refugees from the mainland city of Altinum, during the last years of the western Roman Empire in the fifth century. This settlement was given official sanction in 639 by the Byzantine exarch (governor) of Ravenna, under whose jurisdiction the area fell, and in the same year a basilica was begun, dedicated to Mary the Mother of God. Nothing of this church now survives. What you see at the end of your walk from the edge of what Ruskin so poetically calls 'the wild sea-moor' is an extensively refashioned building dating from the eighth to the eleventh centuries.

The tall façade is varied by a portico running from end to end, under which you pass to enter one of the most striking of all church interiors from the early Middle Ages. The layout is in the form of a broad central aisle of Corinthian columns, leading to a screen surmounted by painted panels and an apse beyond. What everybody loves about the basilica of Torcello (the dedication is now to Santa Maria Assunta) is its grave simplicity, the apparent absence of any distracting adornment, which allows the eye to dwell on the pigeon-grey marble of pillars and panels, with its curious watered-silk effect in the zigzag patterns running across the stone.

In fact this plainness is something arrived at rather than original, and we need not necessarily share Ruskin's belief that the brick walls of the nave above its colonnade, and those of the side aisles covered in cream plaster, were always without some form of decoration. The pavement, in any case, arrests us with its patterning of variegated marbles, a floor which, as William Beckford noted, was 'richer and more beautiful than one could have expected, in a place where every other object savours of the grossest barbarism'. Dividing the sanctuary from the nave is a sort of 'iconostasis' of pictured saints, which actually looks more like one of those mediaeval painted rod screens found in English country churches, and does indeed belong to the early fifteenth century.

Behind this, and separated also by some boldly carved stone panels, Byzantine work with characteristic animal, bird and foliage motifs, lies the choir, with its rather ugly semicircle of plain brick seats around a throne. What everyone comes to look at here are the superb mosaics, centred on the severe, black-garbed image of the Madonna as Mother of God (the Greeks call this incarnation 'Theotòka'), with a row of Apostles below her, all bearded with the exception of Saints Philip and Thomas. In the side chapel on the right, Christ himself appears between gorgeously-robed angels, Doctors of the Church beneath him and a further angelic quartet, much more classical-looking in their white robes, heaving high the Mystic Lamb with its halo and cross. On the back wall at the other end of the church is a frantically detailed Last Judgment arranged in five tiers, into each of which the mosaic artists have hardly been able to cram their huge cast of participants.

Next to the cathedral you will discover the finely-proportioned church of Santa Fosca, begun in the twelfth century. The surrounding colonnaded ambulatory opens into a plain brick interior constructed on a Greek cross pattern, but lacking either the dome or the mosaics which would have given it the full Byzantine feeling, probably because the Greeks who originally worked on the project were replaced by native Venetian builders.

From the simple campanile behind these two churches, Ruskin invites us to look down on Torcello and Venice as 'mother and daughter . . . both in their widowhood' (though nowadays you cannot actually climb the tower). The little island is truly a moralizing place, when we consider how important it once was, but we cannot yet declare its neighbouring Venice either dead and gone or even a grieving widow. However slighted, scorned, abused or just misunderstood, the 'miraculous Citty' will endure a little longer – or as long, at least, as human beings still possess the faculty of wonder.

Index

Abbondi, Antonio 125, 151
Accademia Gallery 17, 86, 156–60
Ala Napoleonica 21, 39
Albergo Danieli (Palazzo
  Dandolo) 79
Albergo Paganelli 80
Alberti, Leon Battista 179
Alexander III, Pope 31, 32, 96
Allsop, Susan Mary 70, 71
Amigoni, Jacopo 117
Anafesto, Doge Paoluccio 6, 168
Antenori, Doge Obelerio de' 168
Archivio dello Stato 131
Arsenal 95–7
Ateneo Veneto 44
Athanasius, Saint 81

Bacino di San Marco 78, 96
Balestra, Antonio 117
Balla, Giacomo 161
Bandiera, Attilio and Emilio 100
Barbara, Saint 85
Barbaria delle Tole 93
Barbaro family 42, 46
Barbaro, Doge Agostino 182
Barbaro, Antonio 43
Barthel, Melchior 128
Basaiti, Marco 157
Baseio, Piero 32

Bassano, Jacopo 173
Battuti di San Rocco 125
Beauharnais, Eugène de 156
Beckford, William 110, 186
Beistegui, Carlos 70, 71
Bella, Gabriele 83
Bellini, Giovanni 10, 40, 44, 56,
  63, 81, 83, 86, 101, 114, 130,
  157, 182
Bellucci, Antonio 99
Benoni, Giuseppe 165
Berenson, Bernard 82, 129
Berlioz, Hector 178
Bessarion, Johannes 38
Betjeman, John 49
Biennale 100, 139
Biblioteca Marciana 38–9
Boccioni, Umberto 161
Bon, Bartolomeo 22, 32, 62, 74,
  125, 129
Bon, Giovanni 32, 74, 129
Bonaventuri, Pietro 136
Bonazza, Giovanni 92
Bordoni, Faustina 72
Boschetti, Lorenzo 161
Bozzetto, Jacopo 171
Bragadin, Marcantonio 92
Braque, Georges 161
Bridge of Sighs 37

Britten, Benjamin 176
Bronson, Katharine de Kay 143, 160
Brosses, Charles de 29
Brown, Rawdon 162
Browning, Robert 52, 143, 165, 185
Brusaferro, Girolamo 46
Brustolon, Andrea 66, 125, 142, 144
Bucentaur (state barge) 95–6
Buora, Giovanni Antonio di 175
Burano (island) 167, 182–5
Burney, Charles 93
Byron, Lord 1, 17, 33, 35, 176, 177

Ca'Dario 18, 162
Ca'Foscari (University) 139–41
Ca'Grande dei Frari 131
Ca'Michiel 153
Ca'd'Oro 74–5
Ca'Pesaro 114–15
Ca'Rezzonico 141–6
Caffi, Ippolito 115
Caliari, Carletto 149
Calle:
  degli Albanesi 79
  Bianca Cappello 136
  di Borgoloco 86
  del Caffetier 93
  del Capitello 64
  Castelli 86
  della Chiesa 82
  del Cimitero 94
  Colonna 71
  del Cristo 71
  Dona 94
  del Dose 100
  Francesco 93
  Largo 61
  Loredan 64
  Lunga 152
  Magno 94

  del Malvasio 65
  della Mandorla 50
  XII Marzo 42
  del Megio 118
  delle Muneghette 94
  Pesaro 115
  dei Proverbi 57
  Racchetta 61
  delle Rasse 79
  della Regina 112, 113
  del Tintor 118
  Vallaresso 41
  Vendramin 73
  Zen 93
Campanile 24–6
Campiello degli Squellini 141
Campo:
  Bandiera e Moro 100–101
  della Celestia 94
  dei Gesuiti 57–60
  del Ghetto Nuovo 65–8
  della Guerra 54
  Manin 50
  dei Mori 61–2
  Nazario Sauro 120
  Saint' Angelo 45, 47, 50
  Saint' Aponal 135
  San Barnaba 146, 152
  San Bartolomeo 51–2
  San Fantin 43
  Santa Fosca 73
  San Geremia 68
  San Giacomo dell'Orio 119
  San Giovanni e Paolo 87, 88–93
  San Lio 54
  San Luca 51
  Santa Margherita 147
  Santa Maria Formosa 84–6
  Santa Marina 86
  San Pantalon 123–4
  San Polo 134–5
  San Rocco 132
  San Stae 115

San Stefano 47, 115, 122
San Vio 160
San Zaccaria 80, 82
Canal, Giambattista 169
Canale della Giudecca 155, 156, 162
Canaletto (Antonio Canale) 77, 78, 159, 165
Candi, Giovanni 51
Candiano II, Doge Pietro 86
Cannaregio district 6, 61–76, 94, 138
Canova, Antonio 97, 128
Cantacuzeno, John 46
Cappella, Francesco 169
Cappello, Admiral Vettor 98
Carlevaris, Luca 78, 144
Carona, Giovanni Antonio 179
Carpaccio, Vittore 16, 40, 102, 157, 159–60
Carriera, Rosalba 159
Casa Alvisi 143
Casa Molin 44
Casanova, Giacomo 38
Casati, Marchesa 162
Casino degli Spiriti 64
Cassa di Risparmio 51
Cassian, Saint 112
Castagno, Andrea del 81, 82
Castello district 139
Catena, Vincenzo 114
Cavalli, Francesco 10, 113
Charles VI, Emperor 106
Chrysostom, Saint John 55, 56
churches:
  Angelo Raffaele 150
  Gesuiti 58–60, 93
  Madonna dell'Orto 62–4
  Sant' Alvise 64
  Sant' Angelo 45
  Sant' Antonio 102
  Santissimi Apostoli 57, 74, 75
  San Barnaba 146

San Biagio 100
San Cassiano 110–12, 113
Santa Caterina 61
Sant' Elena 98
San Fantin 44
San Francesco della Vigna 93–4
Santa Fosca 73
San Geminiano 21
San Geremio 15, 68
San Giacomo dell'Orio 119–20
San Giacomo di Rialto 110
San Giorgio dei Greci 103–4
San Giorgio Maggiore 75
San Giovanni in Bragora 100–101, 102, 136, 138
San Giovanni Decollato 119
San Giovanni Elemosinario 136–7
San Giovani Gristostomo 55–6, 71
San Giovanni in Oleo 82
San Giovanni e Paolo (San Zanipolo) 83, 90–92, 122, 127, 128, 158, 159, 177
Santa Giustina 93
San Gregorio 162
San Lorenzo 103
San Marco, Basilica of 18, 24, 26–31, 174; atrium 31–2; bronze horses 29; façade 28–9; iconostasis 31; mosaic work 30; Pala d'Oro 31
San Marcuola 71–2, 123
Santa Maria del Carmelo (Carmine) 147
Santa Maria della Fava 54
Santa Maria Formosa 84–6, 98
Santa Maria del Giglio 42–3, 162
Santa Maria Gloriosa dei Frari 90, 127–31
Santa Maria Mater Domini 113–14
Santa Maria dei Miracoli 86–7

Santa Maria del Rosario (Gesuati) 155–6
Santa Maria della Salute 18, 22, 68, 139, 163–5
Santa Maria della Visitazione 104
San Martino 95
San Moise 41–2
San Nicolò dei Mendicoli 149–50
San Niccolo da Tolentino 121–3
San Pantaleon e Santa Juliana 123–4
San Pietro di Castello 27, 86, 98–9
San Polo 134
San Rocco 124–6
San Salvador 51, 75
San Sebastiano 151–2
San Simeone Profeta (San Simon Grande) 120–1
San Simon Piccolo 121
San Stae 115–17
San Stefano 45–7, 48, 119
San Toma 132
San Trovaso 153–4
San Vidal 47, 115, 122
San Zaccaria 22, 80–2, 103
San Zulian (Giuliano) 53, 54, 85
Cicogna, Doge Pasquale 16
Cimarosa, Domenico 45
Cini, Count Vittorio 175
Clary, Prince Alphonso 153
Clement XIII, Pope 143
Coducci, Mauro 21, 24, 56, 72, 80, 81, 85, 87, 131, 178, 179
Colbert, Jean Baptiste 184
Colleoni, Bartolomeo 87–8
Colonna, Girolamo Mengozzi 70
Cominelli, Andrea 68
Conegliano, Cima da 63, 101, 147
Constantius, Emperor 29
Contarini family 8
Contarini, Doge Domenico 27

Contarini, Marino 74
Contini, Francesco 150
Contino, Antonio di Bernardino 37, 52
Cooper, Lady Diana 71, 162
Corbellini, Carlo 68
Cornaro family 8
Cornaro, Caterina 52, 57, 112
Corona, Leonardo 149
Corradini, Antonio 41, 115, 147
Correr Museum 39–41, 96, 115, 161
Corti del Milion 55
Corvo, Baron (Frederick Rolfe) 135, 179
Coryate, Thomas 21, 24, 66–7, 88, 90, 113
Council of Ten 8, 35, 118
courtesans 112–13
Cozzi, Marco 129
Credi, Lorenzo di 83
Crosato, Giovanni Battista 142

Da Ponte, Antonio 16
Dal Niel, Signor 79
Dali, Salvador 161
Dandolo, Doge Andrea 30, 31
Dandolo, Doge Enrico 7, 24, 28, 29
Dante Alighieri 36, 95
Dario, Giovanni 162
Diaghilev, Sergei 179
Dickens, Charles 79
Diocletian, Emperor 29, 123
Diziani, Gaspare 47
Doges' Palace 32–8; Porta della Carta 32–3, 46; Retrostanza dei Capi 37; Sala del Collegio 36–7; Sala del Maggior Consiglio 36; Sala del Quarantia 37; Sala dello Scrutinio 37; Scala dei Censori 35; Scala dei Giganti 33–5; Scala d'Oro 35

Donà, Doge Leonardo 173
Donatello 130
Donatus, Saint 181
Donizetti, Gaetano 44
Dorsoduro district 6, 139–66

Eliot, George 85
Emo, Admiral Angelo 96
Ernst, Max 161
Eustace, Saint 115, 117
Evelyn, John 2, 52, 113

Faenza, Francesco da 81, 82
Falier, Doge Marin 33–5, 119
Falier, Ordelafo 172
Fantoni family 125
Fattoretto, Giovanni Battista 58
Ferdinand I of Austria, Emperor
    128
Ferrara, Leonello d'Este, Marquis
    of 16
Ferrara, Niccolo d'Este, Marquis
    of 119
Festa della Sensa 96
Festa dell' Unità 134
Fini, Vincenzo 41
Florian's (café) 22–4, 39
Fondaco dei Tedeschi 75
Fondaco dei Turchi 118–19
Fondamenta:
    di Cannaregio 68
    del Megio 119
    della Misericordia 61
    Nuove 60, 173
    degli Ormesini 65, 67
    dei Sartori 57
    della Sensa 64
Fondazione Giorgio Cimi 175
Fontebasso, Francesco 60, 125,
    150, 184
food 107–9
Fortunatus 71
Fortuny y Madrazo, Mariano 50

Foscari family 8
Foscari, Doge Francesco 33, 140
Foscari, Jacopo 33, 140
Foscarini, Jacopo 147
Franchetti, Baron 74, 75
Francis of Assisi, Saint 185
Francis II, Emperor 11
Franco, Veronica 149
Frederick I, Barbarossa 31–2
Fumiani, Giannantonio 123, 124

Gabrieli, Andrea 10
Gabrieli, Giovanni 10
Gai, Antonio 25
Galerius, Emperor 29
Galiari, Paolo 151
Galuppi, Baldassare 184–5
Gambello, Antonio 80, 97
Gautier, Théophile 61, 160, 178
George III 174
Ghetto 65–8
Giordana, Luca 99
Giorgione, Il 10, 56, 75, 157, 165
Giovane, Palma 53, 85, 149
Girò, Anna 105
Giudecca (island) 65, 78, 138, 148,
    155, 168–71; Le Zitelle church
    153, 171; Redentor 169–70; San
    Biagio 169
Giustinian, Saint Lorenzo 99
glass-blowing 180
Goethe, Johann Wolfgang von
    13–14, 29
Goldoni, Carlo 3, 11, 132–4
Goncourt, Edmond and Jules de
    61
gondolas and gondoliers 12–14, 154
Gorki, Arshile 161
Grado 4
Gran Teatro della Fenice 43–5
Grand Canal 12, 14–18, 112, 114,
    115, 118, 120, 121, 132, 139,
    142, 148, 156, 162

Grevenbrock, Jan 68
Grigi, Gian Giacomo de' 17
Grigi, Guglielmo 22, 179
Guardi, Francesco 77–8, 103, 144, 150, 159
Guardi, Giannantonio 144, 150, 159
Guggenheim, Michelangelo 161
Guggenheim, Peggy 18, 161

Hale, Sheila 139
Handel, George Frideric 55, 71
Hardrada, Harald 97
Hare, Augustus 31, 40, 124
Harry's Bar 41, 70
Hasse, Johann Adolf 71–2
Heinz, Josef 44
Helen, Saint 98
Henri III of France 95
Hermagoras 71
Honour, Hugh 114, 157
Hotel Bauer Grunwald 42
Howell, James 170
Howells, William Dean 60

Isidore, Saint 30, 174

James, Henry 2, 18, 47, 56, 80, 103, 127, 165, 175
Jews 65–7
John the Almsgiver, Saint 101, 136
John the Baptist, Saint 100, 130
John Palaeologos III, Emperor of Byzantium 119
Joseph II, Emperor 143
Jubanico famiy 42

Kandinsky, Vasily 161

La Grazia (island) 177
La Masa, Giuseppe 114
Lambert, Kit 162
Law, John 42

Lees-Milne, James 144
Lido 6, 175–6
Loggetta 25–6
Lombardo, Pietro 33, 86, 87, 91, 129, 131
Lombardo, Sante 103
Lombardo, Tullio 51, 57, 91
Longhena, Baldassare 10, 22, 66, 86, 93, 99, 114, 128, 163–4, 174, 175
Longhi, Alessandro 83
Longhi, Pietro 84, 144
Loredan family 140
Lotto, Lorenzo 91, 119–20, 147, 158
Lucy, Saint 68

Macaruzzi, Bernardino 125
McCarthy, Mary 170
Maffei, Francesco 144
Maggior Consiglio 8, 11, 36
Magnus, Saint 85
Magrath, Cornelius 145
Malamocco 4, 6, 176
Malamocco, Buono di 27
Malevich, Kasimir 161
Malibran, Maria 55
Malipiero, Doge Pasquale 91
Manin, Daniele 38, 50
Mann, Thomas 176
Mantegna, Andrea 75, 83
Manuel I Comnenus, Emperor 7
Manutius, Aldus 39, 51
Marcello, Doge Niccolò 91
Marchiori, Giovanni 125
Marcolini, Francesco 181
Margutti, Domenico 120
Marini, Marino 161
Mariotti, Giovanni Battista 117
Mark, Saint 27, 31
Masegne, Jacobello 31, 62
Masegne, Jacopo delle 127
Masegno, Pierpaolo 31, 62

194

Masegne, Pietro 127
Massari, Giorgio 71, 104, 131, 142, 155
Mastelli, Rioba, Sandi and Alfani 62
Mauro, Romualdo 179
Maximilian, Emperor 29
Mazza, Giuseppe 170
Mazzorbo (islet) 182
Mechitar, Manug 177
Medici, Bianca de' 136
Medici, Cosimo de' 172
Medici, Francesco de' 136
Medici, Lorenzino de' 134
Memmo, Lorenzo Giustiniani 181
Memmo, Theodore 181
Menescardi, Giustino 46, 117
Merceria 52
Merceria di San Zulian 52–3
Meredith, George 148
Messina, Antonella da 40
Mestre 3
Meyring, Heinrich 41, 43
Michelozzi, Michelozzo 172
Michiel, Doge Domenico 30, 174
Michiel, Doge Vitale 79
Migliori, Francesco 41
Miller, Anna Lady 96
Mocenigo, Alvise 115
Monopola, Bertolomeo 33
Montemezzano, Francesco 149
Monteverdi, Claudio 10, 113, 130
Montin restaurant 152
Moore, Dr John 95
Morlaiter, Giovanni Maria 71, 125, 145, 155, 169
Moro, Domenico 100
Morosini family 171, 172
Morosini, Doge Francesco 43, 97, 122, 164
Morris, James 179
Moryson, Fynes 109
Mulino Stucky 155

Murano (island) 60, 180–2
Museo Storico Navale 96
Musset, Alfred de 79–80, 135, 169

Napoleon 3, 11, 15, 21, 44, 96, 141, 144
Negroponte, Antonio da 94
Nicholas, Saint 150

Ospedale della Pietà 104–5
Ospedaletto 93

Pacifico, Fra (Scipione Bon) 127
Pagello, Pietro 79
Paisiello, Giovanni 44
Palazzo:
  Barbaro 18, 47
  Benzon 17
  dei Camerlenghi 110
  Cappello 120
  Cavalli 18, 156
  Centani 132–4
  Coccina Tiepolo 17
  Contarini dal Bolvolo 51
  Contarini dal Zaffo 64, 156
  Corner 124
  Corner Mocenigo 135
  Dandolo (Albergo Danieli) 79
  Doria 84
  Duodo 45
  Giustinian 140
  Gradenigo 120
  Grimani 17
  Gritti Badoer 100
  Labia 68–71
  Loredan 48
  Marcello Pindamonte Papadopoli 86
  Mocenigo 17, 117
  Pesaro degi Orfei 50
  Priuli 84
  Priuli Stazio 118
  Querini Stampalia 82–4

Sceriman 57
Soderini 100
Vendramin Calergi 72
Venier dei Leoni (Guggenheim
    Gallery) 161–2
Vitturi 84
Zenobia 148
Palladio, Andrea 16, 36, 39, 93, 99,
    121, 153, 155, 169, 172–3, 175
Palmieri, Giuseppe 119
Pantaleon, Saint 123
Paolin café 48
Parodi, Filippo 122
Partecipazia, Doge Angelo 171
Partecipazia, Doge Giustiniano
    168
Paul, Saint 134
Pellegrini, Giovanni Antonio 144
Pellegrini, Girolamo 99
Pellico, Silvia 38
Pepin, King 6
Pesaro, Doge Giovanni 128
Pesaro, Jacopo, Bishop of Paphos
    128
Petrarch 30, 38
Petruccio di Assisi, Fra 105
Piazatta 38, 78
Piazza San Marco (Saint Mark's
    Square) 19–41, 80, 88
Piazzale Roma 139
Piazzatta, Giovanni Battista 54, 91,
    117, 144, 156
Picasso, Pablo 161
Piombo, Sebastiano del 56
Pisani, Francesca Tron 130
Pisano, Andrea 121
Pisano, Nicola 121, 127
Pittoni, Francesco 41
Pittoni, Giambattista 41, 117
Pius VI, Pope 143, 174
Pius VII, Pope 174
Pollock, Jackson 161
Polo, Marco 55, 103

Ponte:
    dell'Accademia 18, 156
    della Cortesia 50
    Foscari 139
    della Frescada 124
    delle Guglie 68
    della Paglia 79
    dei Pugni 147, 153
    del Rialto 15, 16, 109–10, 137
    San Barbara 141
    degli Scalzi 15
    dei Sospiri (Bridge of Sighs) 37
    Storto 136
Pordenone (Giovanni Antonio
    Sacchiense) 136
Pound, Ezra 179
Pozzoli, Gioacchino 134
Procuratie 21–2, 24, 39
Proust, Marcel 79
Punta della Dogana 165

Querini family 82, 109
Querini, Giovanni 83
Querini Benzon, Countess Marina
    17

Rangone, Tommaso 53
Reynolds, Sir Joshua 129
Rezzonico, Faustina 143
Rezzonico, Ludovico 143
Rialto 6, 75, 135, 136
Rialto Bridge (Ponte del Rialto)
    15, 16, 109–10, 137
Ricci, Marco 158
Ricci, Sebastiano 117, 125, 147,
    156, 173
Riccio, Il (Andrea Briosco) 74
Rio:
    delle Eremite 152
    Malpaga 152
    Marin 120
    dei Mendacanti 87
    di San Lorenzo 103

Terra Antonio Foscarini 160
Terra San Leonardo 71
Ritchie, Anne Thackeray 128
Riva Ca' di Dio 100
Riva degli Schiavoni 78, 100, 104
Rizzo, Antonio 33, 98
Roch, Saint 124–5
Romano, Marco 120
Rossi, Domenico 58, 115
Rossi, Giustina 54
Rothko, Mark 161
Rovetta, Giovanni 113
Rubini, Agostino 16
Ruga Bella 120
Ruga di Speziali 110
Ruga Vecchia 136
Ruskin, Effie 20, 62, 63, 79
Ruskin, John 20, 28, 40, 41, 62, 63,
    79, 85, 87, 102, 119, 126, 127,
    140, 160, 165, 186, 187

Sacchini, Andrea 93
St Didier, Limojon de 113
Salizzada:
    dei Greci 103
    del Pistor 57
    Sant' Antonin 102
    San Lio 54
    San Moise 41
    San Pantalon 123
    San Provolo 82
    San Stae 117
Salviati, Giuseppe 126, 164
Salvini-Donatelli, Fanny 44
San Clemente (island) 177
San Francesco nel Deserto (island)
    185
San Giorgio Maggiore (island) 18,
    78, 170, 171–5
San Lazzaro (island) 177
San Marco district 6
San Michele (island) 60, 64, 87,
    178–80

San Nicolò district 149
San Polo district 6
San Servolo (island) 177
Sand, George 79–80
Sanmicheli, Michele 17
Sansovino, Jacopo 21, 25, 31, 32,
    33, 38, 51, 52, 53, 61, 87, 114,
    118, 130
Santa Croce district 6
Santacroce, Gerolamo da 95, 184
Sanudo, Marin 118
Saraceni, Carlo 170
Sardi, Giuseppe 42, 51
Sarpi, Pietro Paolo 73
Scalfurotto, Giovanni 121
Scamozzi, Vincenzo 10, 16, 22, 51,
    121
Scuola:
    dei Calafati 46
    Canton 66
    del Carmine 147–8
    Grande di San Marco 87, 158
    Levantina 66
    Nuova della Misericordia 61
    di San Giorgio degli Schiavoni
        102–3
    di San Giovanni Evangelista 22,
        131
    di Sant' Orsola 159
    di San Rocco 126–7, 131
    Spagnola 66
    Tedesca 66
    dei Varotari 147
Selva, Antonio 43
Sestieri district 6
Shelley, Percy Bysshe 176
Simeon, Saint 120–1
Smeraldi, Francesco 99
Soccorso 149
Society of Jesus 58
Soli, Giuseppe 21
Solimena, Francesco 125
Spavento, Giorgio 51

Stock, Saint Simon 148
Strada Nova 73, 75
Stravinsky, Igor 179
Strozzi, Bernardo 122
Stuart, Henry Benedict 174
Symonds, John Addington 108

Taglioni, Marie 74
Tarsia, Antonio 115
Teatro Goldoni 51
Teatro Malibran 54–5
Teatro del Ridotto 41
Tedesco, Zuan 124
Temanza, Tommaso 73, 121
Theodore, Saint 26, 38
Tiberio, Fra 62
Tiepolo, Bajamonte 53, 82, 109,
  160
Tiepolo, Giovanni Battista 11, 36,
  54, 57, 64, 70, 83, 94, 104, 117,
  134, 143, 144, 145, 148, 155–6,
  159, 184
Tiepolo, Giandomenico 134
Tiepolo, Doge Lorenzo 102
Tintoretto, Domenico 63
Tintoretto, Jacopo 10, 36, 37, 46,
  62, 63, 71, 112, 120, 125, 126–7,
  154, 158, 173
Tintoretto, Marietta 63
Tirali, Andrea 92, 122
Titian 10, 36, 52, 60, 75, 128–9,
  136, 160
Tommaseo, Niccolo 48
Torcello (island) 4, 167, 185–8
Torcello, Rustino da 27
Torre dell' Orologio 24
Torrer, Teodoro 39–40
Tremignon, Alessandro 41, 68
Trollope, Thomas Adolphus 23
Turner, J. M. W. 165

University (Ca' Foscari) 139–41
Ursula, Saint 159

Valier, Doge Bertuccio 92
Valier, Dogaressa Elisabetta
  Querini 92
Valier, Doge Silvestro 92
Van Someren, Dr 135
vaporetti 13
Vasari, Giorgio 82, 88, 127
Vassilacchi, Antonio 173
Vecchio, Palma 85
Venice in Peril Fund 26, 62
Venier, Antonia 64
Venier, Doge Antonio 64
Venier, Doge Francesco 52
Venier, Doge Sebastiano 37
Verdi, Giuseppe 33, 44
Veronese, Carletto 124
Veronese, Paolo 10, 36–7, 70, 91,
  120, 124, 126, 151–2, 158, 170,
  173
Verrocchio, Andrea 83, 88
Vignola, Giacomo da 16
Visconti, Luchino 176
Vittoria, Alessandro 35, 75, 92, 94,
  128, 134, 173
Vitturi, Margherita 179
Vivaldi, Antonio 11, 105–6
Vivarini, Alvise 40, 170
Vivarini, Antonio 124
Vivarini, Bartolomeo 46, 85, 130,
  169

Wagner, Cosima 72
Wagner, Richard 72, 79, 140
Wotton, Sir Henry 67, 73
Wullekopf, Ernst 155

Zaïs, Giuseppe 144, 158
Zandomeneghi, Luigi and Pietro
  128
Zanetti, Anton Maria 159
Zattere 138, 154–66, 168
Zelotti, Giambattista 150
Zen, Francesco 60

Ziani, Marco 93
Ziani, Doge Sebastiano 172

Zompini, Gaetano 68
Zuccarelli, Francesco 144, 158